FOUGHT LIKE DEVILS

THE CONFEDERATE GUNBOAT McRae

Neil P. Chatelain

authorHOUSE®

AuthorHouse™
1663 Liberty Drive
Bloomington, IN 47403
www.authorhouse.com
Phone: 1-800-839-8640

Published by AuthorHouse 6/12/2014

ISBN: 978-1-4969-1531-3 (sc)
ISBN: 978-1-4969-1530-6 (e)

Library of Congress Control Number: 2014909683

TABLE OF CONTENTS

TABLE OF ILLUSTRATIONS

ACKNOWLEDGMENTS

THIS BOOK BEGAN SEVERAL YEARS ago while I was enrolled in a class on the history of New Orleans while an undergraduate at the University of New Orleans. My professor gave an assignment to write a five page paper on a topic related to the history of New Orleans that interested us. I had been studying the Confederate Navy at the time and became determined to write my paper on the *CSS McRae*. A five page paper quickly turned into fifty-two. My professor actually encouraged me to continue my research. He helped me get the chance to present my research at the fifty-first meeting of the Louisiana Historical Association in Monroe, Louisiana in March of 2009. I continued my research on the ship and its crew over the next several years and the final results are presented as this work.

This would not have been possible without the assistance of many others. The librarians and staffs at the libraries at the University of New Orleans, Tulane University, the University of Alabama, the University of Houston, and East Carolina University, In addition, I would like to thanks the employees and volunteers at the National Archives, Library of Congress, the Young-Sanders Center of Franklin, Louisiana, and Memorial Hall in New Orleans. Their help has been instrumental in finishing my research. Finally, I would like to thank my friends and family who helped keep me on track with their encouragement. Most of all, I want to thank my wife Brittany for encouraging me and for assisting me in research, editing, and being there with her loving support.

PROLOGUE

I T WAS AN EARLY MORNING in April of 1862. The sun had not yet risen on the Mississippi River south of New Orleans. The temperature and humidity were already high and smoke covering the area did nothing to comfort the men gathered on deck standing beside their large cannons or those down in the engine rooms. The fight for control of the city of New Orleans was at hand. Among the ships gathered was a Confederate gunboat taking part in the defense of the river. A salvo of shots burst from a Union warship not far away aimed at the Confederate gunboat. One of the shells struck the hull of the ship and started a fire below-deck. The ship's captain immediately dispatched his executive officer to take a detail of men below to contain the fire, which would be disastrous if allowed to spread to the ship's magazine. Regaining focus on the ongoing battle, the captain maneuvered the ship and ordered his gunners to fire a broadside at the enemy ship which was just a couple hundred yards away. The shooting continued for several minutes before the Union ship began to overtake and pass the gunboat, firing one last shot before departing; the cannon was loaded with a canister round, turning the cannon into a massive shotgun. The rounds burst across the weather-deck of the Confederate gunboat, splintering wood and smashing into anything on deck. Suddenly the commanding officer was lying on the quarterdeck clutching two wounds; the pilot directing the steering of the ship lay wounded beside him. The helmsman suddenly cried out that the steering mechanism was not responding. The ship began to drift to the riverbank. The executive officer, just twenty-one years old, was summoned from dealing with the fire below-deck to take command of the ship. For the *CSS McRae*, it was a defining moment that would test the limits of the ship and its crew. Quickly surveying that the ship was in dire straits, the executive officer made a bold move, ordering the steering to be quickly repaired. He then backed the ship off of the riverbank and directed it to steam upriver into the thick smoke, towards the Union ship that had just wounded his captain. The fight for New Orleans was not over yet.

CHAPTER ONE

Mexican Flagged

T HE STORY OF THE *CSS McRae* begins not with the Confederate States
of America, nor even the United States. Instead it begins with Mexico
and the Reform War that took place from 1857-1861. During this
conflict in Mexico the *McRae*, originally known as the *Marquis de la
Habana*, would receive her baptism of fire and first oppose the United
States.

By 1857, the conservative movement in Mexico had gained enough
strength to take up arms and begin a full scale rebellion against the liberal
Mexican government. The conservative movement wished to limit the
expanding ideas in the government of forming a more democratic and
federalist way of governing. Some conservatives even wished for a return of
the monarchy of Spain. When the liberal government made a move to strip
the Catholic church of most of its power, the conservative faction took up
arms and, in bitter fighting, forced the liberals out of Mexico City. They
took refuge in the port city of Veracruz and began to fortify the city from
an inevitable conservative assault.

General Miguel Miramon formed an army of conservatives and began
a march to Veracruz. His intent was to capture the city and crush what
remained of the liberal government. Miramon was a staunch conservative
who had been imprisoned by American forces during the Mexican-
American War. He was well liked by conservatives; he even received
loans on many occasions from local Mexican Catholic churches. General
Miramon arrived in front of Veracruz and launched his planned assault.
The attack failed, and instead of losing more of his army in another attack,
Miramon became determined to lay siege to Veracruz. Besieging the liberal

forces would save his soldiers as well as allowing Veracruz to be cut off from supplies, while his forces were resupplied from the sea. General Miramon looked to ships to provide the needed supplies and to make the siege complete. He wished to blockade Veracruz, cutting it off from both Mexico and the rest of the world.

General Miramon turned to Rear Admiral Thomas Marin of the Mexican Navy to provide additional support. Admiral Marin favored the conservatives and mutinied from the Mexican Navy, along with many of the sailors under his command. The sailors made their way to Cuba. Upon arriving, Marin was granted safe haven by the Spanish government, and he quickly got to work. Admiral Marin began to stockpile supplies and began recruiting Cuban sailors, in addition to Americans, French, Spanish, and Portuguese to augment his Mexican sailors. The docks of Havana were scoured and several steamships were purchased. By February 1860, five ships were being outfitted by Admiral Marin, the *General Miramon*, the *Marquis de la Habana*, the *Democracy*, the *Union*, and the *Messic*. Newspapers in Havana noted that Marin and his ships have "proved a perfect godsend to the Diarlo de la Marina of this city."[1] The sailors loaded a final cargo of "1,000 14-pound bomb shells, two bronze mortars, 4,000 small arms, and more than 60,000 rations" for the aid of Miramon.[2] Admiral Marin flew his flag from the *General Miramon*, which was armed with a howitzer. The *Marquis de la Habana* was also armed with a howitzer while the other three ships remained unarmed.

The *Marquis de la Habana* was a 688-ton steam-sloop that "was built in Philadelphia in 1859."[3] The New Orleans register of ships noted that the ship held an overall length of 176 feet, a beam of twenty-nine feet six inches, and a depth of fourteen feet. She was powered by sails on her three masts as well as a compound engine that turned her single screw propeller. The engine retained a two cylinder configuration. Her smokestack was positioned between the main-mast and the mizzen-mast. This was quite unusual, for most steam powered ships of the time had their smokestacks located between the fore-mast and the main-mast. In addition, the ship had an auxiliary, or donkey, engine used to power pumps to contain flooding. The *Marquis de la Habana* was equipped with one anchor attached to fifty

---

[1]   "Havana Correspondence," *New Orleans Daily Crescent*, April 19, 1860.
[2]   "The Value of the Prizes," *New York Daily Tribune*, March 27, 1860.
[3]   "The M'Rae," *Philadelphia Inquirer*, November 20, 1861.

fathoms of chain, which is just over three shots of available chain. Her hull was painted solid black.

It was estimated that "the fitting out of the two steamers [*General Miramon* and *Marquis de la Habana*] at Havana cost at least $300,000."[4] There were speculations and accusation behind who was financing Marin's forces. One journalist wrote that "it would not surprise me to find Spain openly attempting to take the part of Miramon and the Church in Mexico."[5] Another editorial commented that Marin's forces were supplied "by the authuority [Sic.] of Spain, sustained by the French Government."[6]

Admiral Marin dispatched his ships individually with orders to rendezvous at Antón Lizardo, just south of Veracruz. Once assembled there, the ships would proceed to land supplies and commence a blockade of Veracruz. However, the liberal government was not sitting idly by waiting for Marin to strike. Admiral Marin's ships were declared pirates by the conservative Mexican government, and all nations were called to assist in their destruction or capture. As a gesture of goodwill, the United States, operating ships in the Gulf of Mexico, moved to crush the labeled pirates.

The *General Miramon* and the *Marquis de la Habana* left Havana together on February 26, 1860. They had a total of two-hundred-fifty men onboard, but not all of them knew of their final destination. Several Frenchmen that had shipped onboard the *General Miramon* did not know the final destination of the ships until after they got underway. The Frenchmen claimed that they signed articles on February 20, 1860 not with the *General Miramon*, but with the *Correo Number One*. The four men claimed that "they did not even know that they carried material of war."[7] To add to this, the two ships left Havana flying the Spanish flag and only raised the Mexican flag once out of sight of the Cuban coast.

On February 28, the third day at sea, the *Marquis de la Habana* developed engine problems and the two ships were forced to pull into Sisal, a port city on the Yucatan Peninsula, for emergency repairs. As they entered Sisal, the *General Miramon* encountered the *Mexico*, a Spanish mail steamer that had recently left Veracruz bound for Havana. As they passed the *Mexico*, the Spaniards onboard "all shouted, 'Hurrah for Miramon.'"[8]

---

[4] "The Two Prize Steamers Libeled," *New Orleans Daily Crescent*, March 29, 1861.
[5] "Havana Correspondence," *New Orleans Daily Crescent*, April 20, 1860.
[6] "The Mexican News at Washington," *New Orleans Daily Crescent*, March 22, 1860.
[7] "Statement of Prisoners," *New York Daily Tribune*, March 27, 1860.
[8] Ibid.

Battle of Antón Lizardo

The two steamers left Sisal on February 29 and Admiral Marin ordered all of his guns mounted in anticipation of a fight. As they approached the Mexican coast, Marin ordered the Mexican flags lowered. The two ships appeared before Veracruz flying no flag and awaiting trouble.

The *General Miramon* and the *Marquis de la Habana* arrived at Veracruz at noon on March 6, 1860. A fortress in the besieged city signaled the two ships to show their colors, but Marin ignored the hail and the two ships continued on to Antón Lizardo. Lying in wait were the American men-of-war *USS Savannah* and *USS Saratoga*, mounting a total of seventy-six guns. Accompanying the warships were two chartered civilian steamers, the *Indianola* and *Wave*, each packed with eighty sailors, marines, and soldiers, but without any armament. American forces were under the command of Commodore Thomas Turner. On land, the fort that had hailed Marin's ships earlier was protecting the approaches to Veracruz, manned by liberal-backed forces, which was within range of the American ships to provide them cover with their cannons.

The *USS Savannah* anchored near the Mexican fort and signaled Marin's ships. Admiral Marin, however, ignored the signals. Commodore Turner, commanding the American force onboard the *Savannah*, then signaled the *Saratoga* and the two civilian steamers to move in and engage

Marin's forces. By the time they were steaming towards the Mexican ships midnight was fast approaching. As the American ships arrived on scene, Marin was signaling Miramon's forces ashore. Several times the *Saratoga* hailed the two Mexican ships asking them to surrender. Finally, the *General Miramon* fired its howitzer at one of the *Saratoga's* small boats. The *Saratoga* responded with a broadside and directed the *Indianola* to board. As the *Indianola* moved towards the *General Miramon*, the *Saratoga* then redirected its fire to the *Marquis de la Habana*.

One shell pierced the *Marquis de la Habana* above the waterline and she immediately surrendered. The shell slammed into the engine room and killed the first engineer, an American that was recruited in Havana. The *Indianola* closed and boarded the *General Miramon*. After coming alongside, however, Admiral Marin's cannon shot the *Indianola's* pilothouse away, and she made an attempt to escape the American ship. The only recorded casualty onboard the *Indianola* in the exchange was her captain, receiving "a slight wound on one of his hands."[9] The *Saratoga* then gave chase. The *Saratoga* came alongside and attempted to board, but the *General Miramon* fought the American sailors off and sailed towards shallow water. The water proved to be too shallow, and she ran aground. As the *Saratoga* approached with more boarding parties, the *General Miramon* also surrendered. After the battle, Commodore Turner told Marin that "You have been guilty of a great outrage. You alone are responsible for this unhappy affair, and upon you rests the responsibility."[10]

One American was killed and about thirty Mexicans were wounded in the fighting. The captured sailors were turned over to the liberal forces in Veracruz. It took two days for the *Marquis de la Habana* to get the *General Miramon* off the ground. Admiral Marin's flagship was then towed to Veracruz by the *Indianola* while the *Marquis de la Habana* towed the *Saratoga* into port, the *Saratoga* being exclusively a sailing sloop while the rest of the ships had engines as well. The rest of Marin's fleet never arrived and General Miramon never received his needed supplies. Veracruz was not blockaded and the liberal government received new support through the United States government.

9   "Arrival at Anton Lizardo: Particulars of the Whole Engagement," *New York Daily Tribune*, March 27, 1860.
10 "Killed, Wounded, and Prisoners: Captain Turner's Interview with Marin," *New York Daily Tribune*, March 27, 1860.

Without the necessary supplies, General Miramon's army was repulsed at Veracruz in a second assault that began on March 15. The *New York Times* reported "that out of 5,000 men, composing his army, Miramon lost 2,000" while "the casualties in Vera Cruz [Sic.] were very trifling."[11] In the end, the liberal government defeated General Miramon and remained in power. The continued instability in Mexico paved the way for Napoleon III of France to land an army of occupation in an attempt to reform a French empire in the Americas. The *USS Preble* transported the captured Mexican sailors to New Orleans, who "behaved themselves in a very subordinate and proper manner since they became such."[12] Marin's sailors were held in the Orleans Parish Prison, but Marin himself was "released on bail of $3000, before the U. S. Circuit Court."[13]

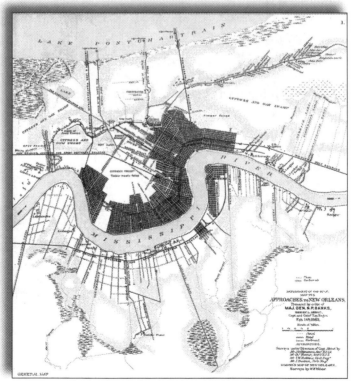

New Orleans during the Civil War

---

11   "Retirement of Miramon from before Vera Cruz" *New York Times*, April 16, 1860.
12   "Naval," *New Orleans Daily Crescent*, March 26, 1860.
13   "The Two Prize Steamers Libeled," *New Orleans Daily Crescent*, March 29, 1860.

The *Marquis de la Habana* was brought to New Orleans where a prize court was convened to decide her fate. However, the court did not rule until after the American presidential election of 1860. Newspapers indicate that "The Mexican prize steamers *Gen. Miramon* and *Marquez* [Sic.] *de la Habana* were sold" on the morning of January 19, 1861.[14] Louisiana would secede from the United States just seven days later. The *Miramon* sold for $12,000 while the *Marquis de la Habana* sold for $20,000. The New Orleans ship register notes that the *Marquis de la Habana* was purchased by Joaquin Loebo. He entrusted the ship to her master, J.C. Smith, who operated her "placed on a line between New Orleans and Havana."[15]

It is known that the *Marquis de la Habana* made at least one round trip to Havana and back to New Orleans. She had apparently run into a storm and her cargo was partially damaged. Upon arriving in Havana, her cargo was "sold at auction."[16] She left Havana on April 10, returning to New Orleans on April 15, 1861. When the ship moored at New Orleans, the crew received word of the firing on Fort Sumter. The outbreak of war would quickly change the history of the *Marquis de la Habana*.

---

[14] "Sale of the Mexican Prize Steamers" *New York Times*, January 21, 1861.

[15] "Letter from John H. Dent, Jr. to John H. Dent", 6 July 1861, *John Horry Dent, Jr., Letters*, University Libraries Division of Special Collections, The University of Alabama.

[16] "Letter From Havana," *New Orleans Daily Crescent*, April 10, 1861.

CHAPTER TWO

Initial Naval Strategy

NEW ORLEANS HAS BEEN AN important city throughout its existence. As the largest population center in the newly formed Confederacy, keeping control of the city would be vital for production of war material and recruitment into the military. As a major seaport, the amount of trade passing through was sorely needed to support the new country. As the dominating position near the mouth of the Mississippi River, New Orleans was the controlling factor to North America's internal water highway. In 1860, there were over thirty-three steamship lines in operation in the New Orleans area alone. Trade in 1860 up and down the Mississippi River, as well as into the Gulf of Mexico to the rest of the world, was valued at $500,000,000. The United States Mint in the city kept a reserve of $500,000 in gold and silver. When Louisiana on January 26 seceded and joined the Confederacy on February 4, 1861, the new government immediately took steps to protect the city from Union military forces. The Confederate Navy was designed to play a major part in protecting the city. One of the ships most involved in the defense of New Orleans for the Confederacy was the *CSS McRae*. The *McRae* took part in battles down the length of the Mississippi River throughout 1861 and 1862, protecting New Orleans and helping to defend the Mississippi River for the new Confederacy.

When the delegates of the seceded states gathered in Montgomery, Alabama in February 1861, they formed the provisional government of the Confederate States of America. One of the first things organized was the Confederate Department of the Navy. Selected to organize and lead the new naval force was Stephen Mallory.

Mallory had served as a United States Senator from Florida in the 1850's and had been a member of the Committee of Naval Affairs. The first goal Mallory put in place was to acquire ships for his new nation, as the Confederacy possessed literally no ships upon its formation. Mallory turned to the larger coastal cities to provide the Confederacy with its first men-of-war. Besides being the largest city in the new Confederacy, New Orleans was also the largest port city in the Gulf of Mexico and was ranked sixth among the largest cities in the United States census of 1860. The city was the closest thing that the Confederacy possessed at its formation to a full naval installation, "having great workshops where machinery of the most powerful kind could be built, and having artisans capable of building ships in wood or iron, casting heavy guns, or making small arms."[17] The contributions from New Orleans to the Confederacy would be vital to the nation's survival. Mallory, recognizing this, immediately sent officials to begin building up naval strength in southern Louisiana.

CSS McRae

On March 15, the new Confederate Congress appropriated funding for ten gunboats. New Orleans, being the nation's largest port, was an obvious choice to start looking for a place to build or acquire them. Mallory dispatched a delegation of three officers, Commodore Lawrence Rousseau, Commander Ebenezer Ferrand, and Lieutenant Robert Chapman, to New

---

17   David D. Porter, "The Opening of the Lower Mississippi," *Battles and Leaders of the Civil War Vol. 2: The Struggle Intensifies*, (New York: The Century Co, 1887), 22.

Orleans. Their goal was to scour the shipyards of the port to determine the feasibility of building the ten gunboats. Their assessment was not promising. Commodore Rousseau wrote to Mallory that there were no immediate facilities to build and outfit warships completely.

He did, however, report that there were three ships that held promise for conversion to men-of-war: the steamers *Yankee*, *Habana*, and *Marquis de la Habana*. The delegation recommended the purchase of these ships which began to be outfitted at Algiers, across the river from New Orleans. The *Yankee* would become the *CSS Jackson*, the *Habana* would be outfitted as the cruiser *CSS Sumter*; the *Marquis de la Habana* was christened the *CSS McRae*. One New Orleans newspaper reported that the Confederate government paid "$53,000 for the Spanish steamer Marquis de [la] Havana [Sic.]."[18]

Secretary Mallory developed an initial naval strategy of building large and powerful ironclad warships capable of breaking the blockade of the Confederacy and crippling the Union fleet. The ironclads would be augmented by smaller and faster wooden commerce raiders. Along with the *Sumter*, the *McRae* was intended to head to sea as one of these commerce raiders.

First Lieutenant Thomas B. Huger

---

18   "Talk on Change," *New Orleans Daily Crescent*, June 28, 1861.

Unlike traditional men-of-war, these ships would actively avoid enemy warships. Instead, they would target the merchant ships of the United States. Their goal was to cripple New England's prosperous shipping and trade industry, causing the wealthy merchants of the northeast to withdraw their support for the war. While the raiders fought the war against the Union's commerce, Mallory's ironclads would smash Lincoln's blockade and take control of the Confederate coastline.

To command the *McRae*, Secretary Mallory selected First Lieutenant Thomas Bee Huger. A native of South Carolina, Huger had been a veteran of the United States Navy for twenty-six years, first joining when he was fifteen years old. His service with the United States Navy included a tour of duty in Veracruz during the Mexican War. He resigned his commission on January 11, 1861 while in the Mediterranean Sea, choosing to cast his lot with his state. Present at the start of the war, Huger was initially stationed in Charleston, South Carolina, "first as inspecting ordinance officer of batteries, then in charge of the batteries of the south end of Morris Island" during the bombardment of Fort Sumter.[19] An officer serving with Huger wrote that he was "an agreeable gentleman, and felt that he was just the man I would like to serve under."[20] Another wrote that "Huger will never give up without a desperate struggle."[21] Huger was a widower, having first married in 1845. His wife, Marianne Meade, was the sister of Union General George Meade. They had five children before her death on December 5, 1857 at age thirty-four. When war began, Huger was engaged to a local New Orleans woman.

---

[19]   "Bombardment of Fort Sumter," *Keowee Courior*, May 18, 1861.

[20]   Charles W. Read, "Reminisces of the Confederate States Navy," *Southern Historical Society Papers*, (Richmond, VA, 1876), Vol. 1, 332.

[21]   "Letter from John H. Dent, Jr. to John H. Dent", 6 July 1861, *John Horry Dent, Jr., Letters*, University Libraries Division of Special Collections, The University of Alabama.

First Lieutenant Alexander F. Warley

Serving as Lieutenant Huger's executive officer was First Lieutenant Alexander F. Warley, another South Carolinian and veteran of the United States Navy whose service dated back to 1840. Warley resigned his commission on December 20, 1860 after South Carolina seceded. He held a reputation in the United States Navy as a strict disciplinarian and his skills would come in handy molding the *McRae's* crew into an effective fighting force. Warley, like Huger, started the war in Charleston, in command of a battery of guns at the Dahlgren Channel during the bombardment of Fort Sumter. Next in the chain of command was First Lieutenant John Eggleston, a graduate of the United States Naval Academy class of 1853 who resigned his commission following the secession of Mississippi on January 13, 1861. First Lieutenant John Dunnington was also a Naval Academy graduate, class of 1855. As a native of Kentucky, he left the United States Navy on April 26, 1861 following the attack on Fort Sumter in the anticipation that his state would soon follow those that had already seceded. Doctor Arthur Lynch from South Carolina, who had been serving in the United States Navy since 1850, reported onboard as the chief surgeon. He resigned from the United States Navy on January 14, 1861. Like Huger and Warley, Lynch was also present at the firing of Fort Sumter, serving as a surgeon to a battery on Morris Island.

Joining these senior officers were several midshipmen. These were junior officers in training or recent graduates from the United States Naval Academy. Passed Midshipman Charles Read was a native of Satartia, Mississippi who graduated from the Naval Academy at Annapolis, Maryland in 1860 at the bottom of his class. He acquired the nickname of "savez" because it was said that this form of the French verb *savoir*, meaning "to know", was the only word that he was able to correctly pronounce during his studies of the language at Annapolis. Read embraced his nickname and would often be heard on deck adding the word to the end of his sentences. Onboard the *USS Powhatan* off the coast of Mexico when he heard of Mississippi's secession, Read resigned on January 19, 1861 and, upon landing in New York City after the *Powhatan* was ordered back to the United States, he immediately travelled to Montgomery, Alabama to personally offer his services to President Jefferson Davis. Acting Midshipmen Sardine Stone of Alabama resigned from the United States Navy on January 14, 1861. Midshipman John Comstock of Arkansas resigned on January 30, 1861. Comstock initially joined the Confederate Army as a first lieutenant, but quickly found an appointment onboard the *McRae* to suit his naval education and training. Midshipman Samuel Blanc of Louisiana rounded out the officers-in-training. Since the Confederacy had no formal naval academy upon its formation and since "some form of education be established for midshipmen", these acting midshipmen were to be instructed on the job by the more senior officers onboard the *McRae*.[22] This form of training remained in place until the Confederacy established a formal academy later in the war on the banks of the James River.

---

[22] *Journal of the Congress of the Confederate States of America*, 1861-1865, Washington: vol. 1, p. 547.

Midshipman Charles W. Read

Assisting the line officers were the staff officers. Leading the engineering department was Chief Engineer Virginius Freeman, a Virginian who had served as a naval engineer since 1851. When Freeman chose to resign from the United States Navy in 1861, his resignation was instead refused and he was dismissed without honor as a way of retaliation against him. This act would be repeated by the United States Navy many times over the coming months. Assisting Freeman was Second Assistant Engineer John Darcy of South Carolina and Third Assistant Engineers Charles Jordan of Virginia and John Dent of Alabama. Other officers would join the ship as it would be fitted out or to replace those onboard who were transferred to other commands. By May 1861, most of the officers had arrived onboard and the crew had been shipped.

Joining the sailors was another unit. Standing next to sailors on men-of-war throughout history was the marines. Colonel Lloyd J. Beall, commandant of the Confederate Marine Corps, was organizing his forces across the South and marine corps recruiting efforts were being focused in New Orleans. Captain A.C. Van Benthuysen began organizing a company of marines in Pensacola, Florida which became Company B,

Confederate States Marine Corps. Captain Van Benthuysen dispatched twenty-four enlisted men from Pensacola to report onboard the *CSS McRae* as their marine detachment. They were led by First Lieutenant Richard Henderson of Virginia. Lieutenant Henderson was the son of the famous former commandant and "Grand Old Man of the Marine Corps," Brevet Brigadier General Archibald Henderson. The *McRae's* marine detachment was accompanied by a detachment of twenty other marines that left Pensacola led by First Lieutenant Becket Howell. These men would be assigned to the *CSS Sumter.* All of these marines had been recruited in New Orleans, Mobile, and Pensacola. Their primary missions onboard were to serve as gunners and aides to the executive officer, the master-at-arms, and the ship's corporal in keeping discipline. These thirty-two men marked the first time in the history of the Confederacy that marines were assigned to warships.

Marines of the time were called to fill many roles. One United States Marine described in his journal what was expected of marines of the time: "one day (or rather one hour) he is a soldier – the next a sailor; and when the ship is going through the process of coaling, he may be found upon the coal whip and be denominated a coal heaver."[23] The marines were officially assigned to the *McRae* on June 27, 1861. With a filling complement of men onboard, Huger now made preparations for getting his ship ready for sea.

The *McRae* was a typical ship that helped to form the new Confederate Navy. She was not originally designed for service as a warship. Instead, the ship had to be modified to accommodate cannon and crew. The men assigned to the *McRae* came from all over the world. Records regarding the makeup of the crew are scattered and incomplete. What records are known, however, paint a picture of warships of the time. At least one-hundred-ninety-seven men are known to have served onboard the *McRae* during its time in the Confederate Navy. Of these, only sixty-one of the crew has records on where they were born or where they lived before the war. The numbers are somewhat surprising to those not familiar with how ships of the nineteenth century were manned. Of those sixty-one men with records of homes, only thirty-one came from a Confederate state. Fourteen were from northern states and another sixteen were from Europe.

---

23   "The Yankee Note-Book Continued," *Galveston Tri-Weekly News*, October 1, 1863.; Henry O. Gusley, *The Southern Journey of a Civil War Marine: The Illustrated Note-Book of Henry O. Gusley* (Austin, TX: University of Texas Press, 2006) 45.

Men from among places like New York, Massachusetts, Maryland, Ireland, England, Scotland, and even one marine from Sweden all served the Confederacy onboard the *McRae*. At least eight men violated England's declaration of neutrality and ignored the Foreign Enlistment Act, shipping onboard the *McRae*. It is impossible to know why each man decided to join the navy and serve on the *McRae*, but there are tendencies that can be looked at. Some men may have been enticed by the prospect of prize money while others only wished for a steady job. Still others may have dreamed of a life of adventure or a way to avoid service in the army. Those from Southern states could have had true ties to the Confederacy or to defending their homes. Even others still may have joined because everyone else was doing likewise. Regardless, the *McRae's* crew now had to work together to survive.

Enlisting was not always easy. James Carr had a tough time joining the Confederate Navy. Born in Brooklyn, New York, he was employed on steamboats travelling the length of the Mississippi River. When the war began, he was "arrested by the New Orleans authorities on suspicion of being a spy, and confined in the [Orleans] Parish Prison for about a month."[24] Released on the good word of his old employer and of a Confederate naval officer, he immediately joined the Confederate Navy, first onboard the *CSS Ivy*, then quickly being transferred to the *McRae*, where he was made the steward of the wardroom. Samuel Hutchinson, Lieutenant Huger's personal clerk, joined the ship after being discharged from the *CSS Sumter* after being declared medically unfit by her commanding officer.

---

[24] *Official Records of the Union and Confederate Navies in the War of the Rebellion* [ORN] (Washington, D.C.: Government Printing Office, 1884 – 1927), ser. 1, vol 19, 626.

CHAPTER THREE

Ship Island

Preparations for getting the *McRae* ready for sea progressed slowly. Secretary Mallory wrote a note to President Davis on April 26, 1861 that informed him of naval activity in New Orleans. He commented that "agents of the department have thus far purchased but two [steamers], which combine the requisite qualities. These, the *Sumter*, and the *McRae*, are being fitted as cruisers and will go to sea at the earliest practicable moment."[25] Jefferson Davis, proud of his small new navy, noted on April 29 in a letter to the people of the Confederacy which was printed in newspapers across the South, that "two vessels have been purchased and manned, the *Sumter* and the *McRea* [Sic.], and are now being prepared for sea, with all possible dispatch."[26] Davis was not alone in documenting the *McRae's* acquisition and fitting out. In New York, newspapers reported that "the steamer *Marquis de [la] Habana* has been purchased by the Southern Confederacy, and will soon be fitted out as a war steamer."[27]

Though New Orleans had built many small merchant ships and tugs in the past, it had never been a major military depot or station for outfitting men-of-war, and there was no shortage of ships being prepared. Newspaper editors were invited to tour the *Washington*, a cutter being outfitted. While touring, the editors also saw "at the ship-yards at Algiers, several other ships of the Confederate States, which are being fitted up with great rapidity and completeness for the service," including the *Sumter*, the *Star of the West*,

---

25 Ibid., Ser. 2, vol 2, 52.
26 "Message from Jefferson Davis," *Shreveport Daily News*, May 11, 1861.
27 "Reports from New Orleans" *New York Times*, April 25, 1861.

and the *McRae*.[28] Lieutenant Huger worked the crew tirelessly to install the ships armament. The *McRae*, when completed, would mount a total of eight guns: six thirty-two pounder cannon in broadside, one nine-inch Dahlgren gun on pivot amidships, and one twenty-four pound brass rifle on pivot. These artillery pieces were sent by rail from Norfolk, Virginia. After Virginia seceded, state authorities captured the Gosport Navy Yard, including one-thousand pieces of artillery and several ships. In the end, some one-hundred-ninety-seven guns would be sent to New Orleans from Virginia to aid in its defense. Approximately one-hundred-thirty to one-hundred-forty officers and enlisted men would be required to maintain a full complement onboard the *McRae*. The number, however, would usually range somewhere "from 100 to 119 men and officers."[29] Commander Raphael Semmes was also in New Orleans. The future rear admiral of the Confederate Navy was, fitting out the *CSS Sumter* at James Martin's Atlantic Dry Dock in Algiers while Huger worked simultaneously with outfitting the *McRae*. Semmes commented on how little New Orleans was prepared to be a major naval base, noting how there was no navy yard for men-of-war to receive supplies and fill orders. Instead, "everything had to be improvised, from the manufacture of a water-tank, to the 'kids and cans' of the berth-deck messes, and from a gun-carriage to a friction-primer."[30]

Though no facilities existed when the war began, New Orleans soon moved to expand its naval industries. Within a few weeks, "a laboratory was established in New Orleans, and authority given for the casting of heavy cannon, construction of gun carriages, and the manufacture of projectiles and ordnance equipments of all kinds."[31] By late 1861, there were three powder mills producing well over five-thousand pounds of gunpowder daily. Half of the Marine Hospital on the southeastern outskirts of the city was converted to into an ammunition factory which would supply the New Orleans area with all of its ammunition needs, as well as creating a large surplus to send to other fronts. The Southern Shoe Factory was producing over two-hundred-fifty pairs of boots daily. Meanwhile, four major iron works and foundries were producing artillery

---

[28]   "Our Little Navy," *The Shreveport Weekly News*, June 3, 1861.

[29]   ORN, ser. 1, vol 18, 249.

[30]   Raphael Semmes, *Memoirs of Service Afloat: During the War Between the States* (Baltimore, MD: Kelly Piet & Co, 1868), 98.

[31]   Jefferson Davis, *The Rise and Fall of the Confederate Government, Volume 2* (New York: Appleton and Co., 1881), 213.

pieces and shipboard necessities such as boilers and engine machinery. New army, navy, and marine installations sprang up in the city each week. In addition, the shipyards at Algiers were packed with gunboats undergoing conversion. Each day the lists of ships undergoing conversion to warships grew at the shipyards of John Hughes and Company, Hyde and McKay, Harrum and Company, and the Atlantic Dry Dock Company.

Newspapers chronicled the ongoing progress of both the *McRae* and the *Sumter*. One New Orleans paper wrote that the *McRae* "is an excellent sea-boat, and is being thoroughly overhauled and strengthened in every part; and will doubtless, under the command of her very efficient officers prove a no mean acquisition to our little navy."[32] However, they typically reported rumors relating to troop movements and naval preparedness. Inconsistencies were commonplace. One Georgia paper listed both the *Sumter* and the *McRae* as privateers, indicating falsely that they were both privately owned. A Connecticut newspaper commented that both the *Sumter* "and the '*McRae*' [would] be sent to Memphis" as soon as they were completed.[33] This was completely opposite to what Mallory intended for the two ships. Added to these commentaries were requests from army officers to have the *McRae* outfitted as soon as practicable. Major General Gideon Pillow, commanding forces in western Kentucky and Tennessee, insisted in a report written on June 20 to the Secretary of War that "if the President has not yet ordered the *McRae* up, let it be done as promptly as possible."[34] General Pillow was concerned with Union forces building up in the area, particularly Union gunboats under construction in Cairo, Illinois. Though the crew did not know for certain what their future would bring, they could make educated guesses. John H. Dent, an engineer onboard, speculated to his father that "I can't imagine where we will go but I suppose we will try and sink the blockade."[35]

As work continued on the docks of the Mississippi River, the *McRae* suffered its first casualty. On June 20, James Keen, a thirty year old native of Ireland died from a fracture to his skull. *The Daily True Delta*, a newspaper in New Orleans, reported that he "fell from the yard-arm of the

---

[32] "The Confederate Navy," *New Orleans Daily Crescent*, May 27, 1861.

[33] "The Latest News by Telegraph," *Hartford Daily Courant*, June 20, 1861.

[34] ORN, ser. 1, vol 22, 789.

[35] "Letter from John H. Dent, Jr. to John H. Dent", 25 June 1861, *John Horry Dent, Jr,. Letters*, University Libraries Division of Special Collections, The University of Alabama.

government steamer *McRae*, and striking a wharf had his skull fractured, and died in consequence thereof."[36] An investigation about Keen's death determined that his fall had been an accident and held no one accountable.

While Lieutenant Huger prepared the *McRae*, many of the crew would be involved in another adventure. Army officials wished for Union gunboats that were patrolling the lakes of coastal Louisiana and Mississippi to be eliminated. The crew of the *McRae* was called upon to help secure the coast. Asked to command the expedition was Lieutenant Alexander Warley, executive officer of the *McRae*. Accompanying Warley was Lieutenant Dunnington, Surgeon Lynch, Paymaster Sample, Midshipmen Read, Stone, and Comstock. Warley also took the *McRae's* marine detachment and approximately eighty sailors and loaded them on two steamers, the *CSS Oregon* and the *CSS J.D. Swain*. Once loaded, they headed towards the last known location of the Union ships. Some Confederate Marines, newly arrived from Pensacola, joined the expedition at the last moment, as well as Midshipmen William R. Dalton and Francis M. Roby, both assigned to the New Orleans naval station. At the time, Roby was the chief commissary officer for the *McRae*. A newspaper in Richmond reported that there were "65 sailors and 85 marines", but the true number was more likely eighty sailors and fifty-five marines.[37]

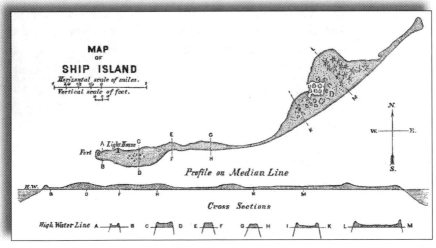

Map of Ship Island

---

36   "Fatal Fall," *The Daily True Delta*, June 21, 1861.
37   "Fight at Ship Island – Particulars of the Engagement," *Daily Richmond Examiner*, July 16, 1861.

USS Massachusetts

The force left New Orleans on July 5, 1861 and made their way to Bay Saint Louis on the Mississippi coast. Once there, Warley had the men load the two ships with sandbags to provide some protection from enemy fire. They left Bay Saint Louis at 9:00 on the morning of July 6 and began to search for Union ships. After searching the sounds and lakes, no enemy was sighted, and Captain Edward Higgins of the Confederate Army who had first proposed the expedition determined that the group should then move to occupy Ship Island, Mississippi. The island was strategically situated in the Gulf of Mexico and was, being the only deep water anchorage between Mobile and New Orleans, the perfect staging point for possible future Union operations in coastal Louisiana, Mississippi, and Alabama. Higgins had been a lieutenant in the United States Navy before the war and resigned from the naval service to serve his native state of Louisiana.

The expedition landed on Ship Island at 4:00 pm on July 6, 1861 and immediately began to fortify the island. This was the first case of the new Confederacy using amphibious and combined operations. Lieutenant Warley brought one thirty-two pounder cannon, one eight-inch cannon, and two howitzers with him on the expedition and he immediately began to mount them in strategic locations while posting a lookout on the island's lighthouse to watch for Union ships. While fortifying the island, the *Oregon* spotted two vessels, but upon further investigation, they proved to be fishing boats. After finding the two fishing boats, the *J.D. Swain* and the *Oregon* left to get reinforcements from New Orleans to provide a permanent garrison for the island. The two ships arrived in New Orleans on the morning of July 7 and sought out reinforcements from army forces in the city. The *Oregon* and the steamer *Gray Cloud* left on July 8 full of men and supplies bound for Ship Island.

Warley ordered his men to place some of his artillery in the old fort that had been under construction by the United States Army, which was never completed. The men dug earthworks to protect the rest of the cannon. On the night of July 8, a Union gunboat, the *USS Massachusetts*, was sighted by Warley's men on the horizon. She proceeded to anchor within a mile of Ship Island. The sailors and marines continued to fortify their positions throughout the night. At dawn, Midshipman Charles Read, on the order of Lieutenant Warley, opened fire upon the *Massachusetts* with the eight-inch gun. One northern newspaper later recounted that "the first shot was fired by the Confederates while the officers [of the *USS Massachusetts*] were at breakfast."[38] The Union ship then replied with its guns, compelling the entire armament of Ship Island to join in. Read later wrote that after about an hour of firing with little effect, "the steamer having [built] steam, withdrew out of range and proceeded out to sea."[39] The long range exchange of artillery fire was short-lived. The *USS Massachusetts* only fired seventeen shots while Warley's men responded with twenty-six. Later in the day, the steamers returned with elements of the Fourth Louisiana Infantry Regiment under Lieutenant Colonel W.H. Allen. In the entire action, the *Massachusetts* fired "some thirty odd rounds of shell and round shot, which sank in the sand," causing no real damage.[40] Only one man suffered a slight leg injury. The *Massachusetts* suffered little damage "except cutting up the rigging somewhat."[41]

Lieutenant Warley's sailors and marines then re-boarded the ships and began the trek back to New Orleans. The crew re-boarded the *McRae* on July 10. The *McRae's* crew had taken part in its first combat operation and had performed well. They suffered only one slight casualty, secured Ship Island for the Confederacy, and pushed back an enemy gunboat. They set a standard that other naval personnel in the area would strive to follow. Captain Higgins later praised Warley and his men in his after action report for their service.

While Warley and most of the crew were taking part in securing Ship Island, the engineering department was busy finishing preparations onboard the *McRae*. Third Assistant Engineer John H. Dent wrote to his father on July 9 that "we will get up steam today in the boilers and connect

---

38   "The Engagement at Ship Island," *Baltimore Sun*, July 26, 1861.
39   Read, 333.
40   "A Naval Brush at Ship Island," *The Shreveport Weekly News*, July 22, 1861.
41   "The Engagement at Ship Island," *Baltimore Sun*, July 26, 1861.

the engine for the first time."[42] The initial tests were successful. Lieutenant Huger now had full use of the engine. The *McRae* was now ready to sail and fight.

Within forty-eight hours of Warley's return, Lieutenant Huger declared the *McRae* fully converted and on July 12, 1861 he ordered the commissioning pendant closed up on the main-mast for the first time. The *McRae* was now a confederate man-of-war and was ready to receive its ordinance stores. To get these, the *McRae* made the trek up the Mississippi River to Baton Rouge, the capital of Louisiana. This would be the first time that the *McRae* would be underway as a Confederate warship. The ship was recorded at being able to move at eight knots, but moved slower upriver against the current of the Mississippi River. The trip upriver did help to provide the crew with their first full taste of service onboard an underway man-of-war.

A typical day onboard was packed full of events. Every morning at daybreak, Boatswain's Mate Thomas Wilson, an Irish immigrant who had made his way to New Orleans, would wake the crew with a trill from his pipe. The men would muster on the deck for a morning inspection of the ship to determine what work needed to be done that day. After the inspection, the men would then have breakfast. Dining on a warship was strictly segregated by rank. Lieutenant Huger would typically dine in his stateroom alone while the officers would eat in the wardroom. Preparing the meals for the officers was Wardroom Cook William Butler, a native of New Jersey. Wardroom Steward James Carr, the Brooklyn New York native who was accused of being a spy, served the officers their food. Warrant Officers dined amongst themselves, dividing further into the engineer's mess and the midshipman's mess. Petty officers would dine with each other and the deck seamen formed their own messes. Each mess was made up of about eight men. The daily job of cooking food was rotated amongst the group while the rest of the mess maintained the ship and stood watches.

Following breakfast, the officers and petty officers would then supervise the cleaning of the ship and the making of any necessary repairs. Carpenter's Mate P.G. Newman would maintain the woodwork and monitor repairs made to the hull and masts. Boatswain's Mate Wilson helped supervise the

---

[42] "Letter from John H. Dent, Jr. to John H. Dent", 9 July 1861, *John Horry Dent, Jr,. Letters*, University Libraries Division of Special Collections, The University of Alabama.

training of the landsmen into more professional sailors as well as helping to supervise the daily maintenance of the ship's lines, small boats, and anchor. Paymaster Sample and Paymaster's Clerk Albright oversaw the payment of the crew and assisted Lieutenant Huger in handling the *McRae's* accounts.

The day was divided into five 4-hour watches and two 2-hour dogwatches. During each watch, a more senior officer was assigned as the officer of the deck. This was typically a lieutenant or a senior ranking master. The officer of the deck recorded things officially in the ship's log and supervised the whole ship on behalf of Lieutenant Huger. When underway, their primary duty was the safe navigation of the *McRae*, but they controlled everything from drills and exercises to when the crew could smoke. The officer of the deck would be assisted by the sailing master and his assistant, Passed Midshipman Charles Read and Quartermaster Thomas Rohman, in the navigation of the ship. At times, a river pilot would also lend his expertise to guide the *McRae*. Lieutenant Warley, being the executive officer, helped to train the midshipmen in navigation and seamanship to prepare them to serve as future officers of the deck.

The engineering department operated the engine, boilers, and single screw propeller that the *McRae* used for propulsion. The engineers, firemen, and coal heavers worked in the engine room, the fire room, and the boiler room. The engineering spaces were located directly below the quarterdeck and a speaking tube ran from the quarterdeck directly below to the engine room. Officers on the quarterdeck would either speak into the tube or ring a bell that the engineers would hear and then respond with the correct orders for the engine. For example, if Lieutenant Huger wished the *McRae* to move at its full eight knot speed, he would order that four bells be made. The officer of the deck would then ring the bell four times to signal full speed ahead. For propulsion, coal was heated to create steam. The steam pressure would build up in the boilers and be used to turn shafts that drove the screw propeller, thus moving the ship forward. The *McRae* preferred to burn an anthracite coal, just as most of the ships of the time. Temperatures in the engineering spaces were usually much higher than the rest of the ship. One engineer recorded that the engine room would usually register at one-hundred-twenty-nine degrees Fahrenheit while the boiler room could even top that, reaching one-hundred-fifty-four degrees at times.

Whenever Lieutenant Huger wished it, drills of all sorts were performed. These ranged from fighting invisible fires to beating back imaginary enemies attempting to board the ship. Drill at the guns was usually the most common. One Civil War sailor recorded in his memoirs that they "were kept busy at these different drills twice each day, or until we became proficient in all. After that we drilled twice a week, and sometimes only once a week were we called upon to drill."[43] Besides drills, the crew worked on everything imaginable. The deck had to be cleaned daily using large stones called holystones, the rigging had to be repaired, the engine and boilers had to be kept in top performance, the cannon had to be cleaned and maintained, supplies on board had to be monitored, and the many items of brass onboard had to be polished. Life onboard the *McRae*, just as any warship, was a constant job of upkeep and maintenance.

Breaking up the constant working was lunch at noon and dinner during the dogwatches between 4:00 and 8:00 pm. Also, twice daily the crew was mustered and each man was issued his ration of grog. In keeping with naval tradition, sailors were issued a gill, about four ounces, of the mixture of whiskey and water known as grog. This tradition began with the British Navy and continued in the American Navy. It was the opinion of the naval service that is was better for the crew to be issued grog than sneak away to get their hands on stronger alcohol. Taps was at 10:00 pm and part of the crew went to sleep while the night watches continued to navigate the ship. If events required Lieutenant Huger and the rest of the ship's attention, the officer of the deck would typically either summon the executive officer or the commanding officer, or simply rouse the whole crew by ordering the drum onboard to sound the beat sending the crew to their general quarter's stations.

On each Sunday, as was the custom in all American, British, and Confederate warships, the crew was mustered together, and the articles of war were read aloud for all to hear. This was a list of the most serious infractions that a sailor could commit, such as theft, sleeping on watch, stealing, and murder. For most of these, the end result was the execution of the convicted sailor. The first time a new sailor heard the articles of war read aloud, they would often become overawed and frightened, but the officers and petty officers who heard them recited every week and never took notice of the infractions. If a case was not covered by the articles of war, then punishment would be determined in a "captain's mast". In this, Lieutenant Huger would hear what a sailor had done and render a punishment appropriate to the infringement. The master at arms or ship's

---

[43] Stephen F. Blanding, *Recollections of a Sailor Boy: or Cruise of the Gunboat Louisiana* (Providence, RI: E.A. Johnson, 1886), 62 – 63.

corporal would monitor the accused and see that the sentence was carried out. Punishments could range from extra duty assignments, denial of liberty ashore, and loss of privileges onboard. One sailor noted that "one mode [of punishment] was to send the man to the mast head for three hours. This was considered a light punishment by the majority. Another was to send the men up the ratlines on the under side [Sic.], in board, and cause them to hang there for two hours."[44] Depending on the commanding officer or his second in command, punishments could be quite harsh.

The *McRae* anchored off of Baton Rouge on July 14 and began to take on munitions from the state arsenal. The arsenal had been captured by secessionists in January 1861 and provided the backbone for arming and outfitting most of the ships at New Orleans, as well as the thousands of volunteers flocking to the army in Louisiana. Among the supplies stored at the arsenal was 50,000 stands of small arms, approximately thirty-five pieces of artillery, over three-hundred barrels of gunpowder, as well as a quantity of artillery and small arms ammunition.

The *McRae* remained in Baton Rouge for several days receiving her munitions. One engineer noted that Lieutenant Huger was pleased with the speed which the ship made the journey to the state capital. The officers supervised the transfer of supplies while David Wiltz, the ships gunner, monitored "the reception on board, and proper distribution, of all ordnance equipment and stores."[45] While in Baton Rouge, a second tragedy took away another member of the crew. On the night of July 14, Third Assistant Engineer Philip Thomas, a native of Maryland, fell overboard while sleepwalking and drowned. His body was never recovered despite a thorough search of the surrounding water. Along with many of the crew, "he took his hammock up on deck on account of the heat below."[46]

While docked at Baton Rouge, one new sailor reported onboard. Midshipman James M. Morgan was young, just fifteen years old when he first stepped onboard the *McRae*. He was a native of New Orleans who was living in Baton Rouge at the time. Following the surrender of

---

[44]   Ibid., 61.

[45]   Confederate States of America Navy Department, *Ordnance Instructions for the Confederate States Navy Relating to the Preparation of Vessels of War for Battle, to the Duties of Officers and Others When at Quarters, to the Ordnance and Ordnance Stores, and to Gunnery* (3rd ed., London: Saunders, Otley and Company, 1864), 9.

[46]   "Letter from John H. Dent, Jr. to John H. Dent", 16 July 1861, *John Horry Dent, Jr., Letters*, University Libraries Division of Special Collections, The University of Alabama.

Fort Sumter, young Morgan left the United States Naval Academy and proceeded to look for a position in the Confederate Navy, first serving briefly transporting munitions from New Orleans to Pensacola. He had spent less than a year at Annapolis. Morgan made himself at home with the junior officers onboard, several of whom he knew from his time at the Naval Academy. James Morgan had been trying for several months to receive an assignment to a Confederate warship; however, no open billets were available in the few ships the navy possessed. Lieutenant Huger welcomed him onboard the *McRae* with open arms. Huger even had dinner one evening with the Morgan family at their house. Within moments of reporting for duty, young Morgan later wrote, he was "sent ashore, on duty, in charge of the first cutter, and how my small heart swelled with pride and how my fellow townsmen's eyes opened with amazement as they heard "little Jimmie Morgan" giving orders to the sailors" to continue the loading of ammunition.[47]

While receiving her ordinance stores, problems with the engines developed and the *McRae* had to make its way back to the docks of New Orleans. Third Assistant Engineer Dent wrote that the ship "had the misfortune to break or crack two of the wheels which drives the propeller shaft."[48] The ship would be unable to properly use her steam propulsion without repairs, which would take several weeks to complete. It is unknown whether Huger and the crew were aware of the engineering trouble that the ship experienced while in Sisal, Mexico as the *Marquis de la Habana*. The engineering problems of her past, however, would continue to reappear in the future. While repairs were in progress, Lieutenant Richard Henderson was transferred back to Pensacola, Florida to serve with the bulk of Company B, Confederate States Marine Corps. Accompanying Henderson was Sergeant John Morgan. Sergeant John Seymour, a native of Delaware, was left in charge of the *McRae's* detachment of Marines.

---

[47]   James Morris Morgan, *Recollections of a Rebel Reefer* (New York: Houghton Mifflin Co, 1917), 53.

[48]   "Letter from John H. Dent, Jr. to John H. Dent", 21 July 1861, *John Horry Dent, Jr., Letters*, University Libraries Division of Special Collections, The University of Alabama.

Midshipman James M. Morgan

While undergoing repairs, Lieutenant Huger anchored the *McRae* across from Jackson Square. His fiancée, whom many considered to be the loveliest women in New Orleans, lived in one of the Pontalba buildings facing the Saint Louis Cathedral in the square. On many occasions, the junior officers would carry notes between Huger and his fiancée. Huger most often assigned this responsibility to young Midshipman James Morgan who would later write that he "carried so many notes from the captain [that] the young lady made such a pet of me."[49]

While the *McRae* sat off of New Orleans making her engineering repairs, Secretary Mallory was preparing the ship for an important mission. Lieutenant Huger received secret instructions from the secretary. In these, he was instructed to escape the blockade and deliver dispatches to Commander James Bulloch in London, England. Huger would then return to the Confederacy full of supplies to help the fledgling navy arm itself. If successful, the *McRae* would be the first Confederate warship to enter a European port.

In the dispatches, Secretary Mallory informed Commander Bulloch of the great Confederate victory at the Battle of Manassas in July of 1861. In addition, Bulloch was instructed that, "if you can purchase 10,000

---

[49]   Morgan, 54.

good Enfield rifles, or rifled muskets with bayonets, do so at once, without regard to price, if they can be brought in the *McRae*."[50] Mallory went further, requesting that in addition to the "muskets to be purchased on account of the Navy and to be sent over on the *McRae*, you will purchase about 200 tons of powder."[51] If Bulloch felt he could after "consultation with Lieutenant Huger, you shall think she can carry more, you will act accordingly and send more."[52] Another dispatch to Bulloch asked whether he had purchased any ships in England. Mallory reasoned that "the *McRae* has good pilots and could sail in company with any such vessel across the ocean to our shores."[53] The crew was not aware of these instructions and all believed they were to solely seek out and destroy Union commercial shipping. No one but Huger, and possibly Lieutenant Warley, knew that their destination would be England.

The repairs continued through the rest of July. By this time, the crew was becoming anxious. The *CSS Sumter* under Commander Raphael Semmes had managed to escape the Union blockade and begin its attack on Union commerce. During the *Sumter's* cruise in the Caribbean Sea and the Atlantic Ocean, she would take eighteen prizes in six months. The *McRae's* sailors wished to do the same thing; the prospect of prize money earned for each capture was enticing. Third Assistant Engineer Dent wrote to his father that "all that our officers wish is to capture and burn every thing that we cannot take."[54]

Young James Morgan wrote of being "mastheaded" while onboard the *McRae*, which consisted of "having to climb up to the cap of the foretopmast and stand there with barely space enough for his two little feet, and he had to hold on to the stays to keep from falling."[55] Morgan then commented that he was often required to climb the mast as he was often caught in one act or another. He recalled one instance specifically where Lieutenant Warley ordered young Morgan to report to Lieutenant

---

50   ORN, Ser. 2, vol 2, 81.
51   Ibid., 82.
52   Ibid., 81.
53   Ibid., 82.
54   "Letter from John H. Dent, Jr. to John H. Dent", 3 August 1861, *John Horry Dent, Jr., Letters*, University Libraries Division of Special Collections, The University of Alabama.
55   Morgan, 54.

Eggleston to be mastheaded. Eggleston replied to Morgan that "Well, sir, you surely ought to know the way up there by this time!"[56]

The *Sumter* was not the only ship capturing Union merchants. Several privateers operating out of New Orleans in the Gulf of Mexico were returning up the Mississippi River with prizes. The *Calhoun* captured six merchants in April and May. These six captures were sold at auction for $28,000. The privateer *Music* captured two ships in May that were sold for a combined total of $50,000. The *Ivy* also made two captures in May. Each word of a new capture made the *McRae's* sailors more anxious to complete their repairs and proceed to sea.

By this time, the Confederate Congress had passed two laws governing privately owned ships attacking Union warships. The first law stated that "the owners of privately armed vessels are entitled to receive, in Confederate bonds, from the Treasury of the Confederate States, twenty percent of the value of any armed public vessel of the United States they may destroy."[57] The second law stated that a bounty of twenty dollars was to be paid "for each prisoner, on board of any armed ship or vessel belonging to the United States" that was captured by a privateer and brought to Confederate authorities.[58] Privateers across New Orleans were looking for a chance to attack Union men-of-war; however, most were too lightly armed to have a chance of beating a fully armed Union gunboat. Their major chances of success would be attacking and capturing Union gunboats that were being converted from merchant ships to help man the blockade.

By August 8, 1861, the repairs were completed and the *McRae* made a trial steam down the Mississippi River. During the journey, engineers discovered that some of the "lugs in the driving wheels tore out" and would have to be replaced.[59] The *McRae* returned to New Orleans to undergo yet more repairs, which would take several days. Once the repairs were complete, the *McRae* left the docks of New Orleans steaming downriver. Secretary Mallory, eager for the *McRae* to get to sea, wrote to President Davis that the *McRae* "is ready and watching for an opportunity to get to sea."[60] However, Union forces believed that Huger had already made an

---

56   Ibid.

57   "The Battle of the Passes," *New Orleans Daily Picayune*, October 14, 1861.

58   Ibid.

59   "Letter from John H. Dent, Jr. to John H. Dent", 10 August 1861, *John Horry Dent, Jr., Letters*, University Libraries Division of Special Collections, The University of Alabama.

60   ORN, Ser. 2, vol 2, 76.

escape into the Gulf of Mexico. The *New York Times* mistakenly reported on August 12 that the "war steamer, the *McRae*, got out to sea yesterday by running the blockade."[61] The sailors onboard knew of this, commenting that "it is now reported in the Northern papers that we have already gotten out."[62]

---

[61] "Notes of the Rebellion; From Fortress Monroe. Movements in Arizona. How it was Done the Cherokees. A Female Spy. The Rebel War Vessels. A John Brown Man." *New York Times*, August 12, 1861.

[62] "Letter from John H. Dent, Jr. to John H. Dent", 10 August 1861, *John Horry Dent, Jr., Letters*, University Libraries Division of Special Collections, The University of Alabama.

CHAPTER FOUR

Head of the Passes

L IEUTENANT HUGER BROUGHT THE *McRae* downriver and anchored it by the army posts Forts Jackson and Saint Philip, on September 1, 1861. These forts were designed to prevent enemy ships from advancing upriver and taking New Orleans by assault. It was at these forts that the ship remained, waiting for a chance to run the Union blockade. A telegraph station had been built connecting the Head of the Passes and Fort Jackson, so Lieutenant Huger knew at all times the location of the Union ships in the area. The *McRae* remained anchored for several days there while the *CSS Joy*, a recently converted warship, provided reconnaissance down to the mouths of the river. While waiting, several engineers displayed their displeasure for the *McRae's* engine, commenting that it was not capable of moving the ship with the speed required of commerce raiders and that it would continue to be a problem to maintain. On several occasions, the Lieutenant Huger prepared to run past the blockade on moonless nights, but "on each occasion the pilots raised objections, saying that the *McRae* drew too much water for them to take the responsibility, or that they were not pilots for the bar of the pass selected."[63]

In late September, the *Joy* spotted a large man-of-war steaming upriver. Charles Read, recently promoted to the rank of master, noted that the *McRae* "went to quarters and awaited under way the report of the *Joy*, which was in advance of the approaching steamer."[64] The vessel proved to be the French gunboat *Lavoisier*, which had passed through the Union blockade as a neutral ship carrying dispatches and as an observer of international

---

[63] Morgan, 53.
[64] Read, 334.

maritime law. It was customary of the time for neutral men-of-war to be allowed to pass through blockades after inspection for contraband. The French naval officers onboard the *Lavoisier* informed Captain Huger that "had grounded in trying to get over the bar; that he saw no blockading vessels until 10 o'clock next day [October 2], when a small side-wheel gunboat called the *Water Witch* arrived off the Pass."[65] The *McRae* proceeded to New Orleans to spread word of the arrival of the *Lavoisier*, which anchored at the forts. Many believed that the French ship could be carrying word of official French recognition of the Confederacy. The *Lavoisier's* officers proceeded to New Orleans onboard the steamer *Watson*. As the *Watson* and her embarked French officers arrived at the city on September 25, they "received a salute of five guns" from the *McRae*.[66] The French ship was not there to announce recognition and soon afterwards, Lieutenant Huger returned the ship to the forts to await his chance to run the blockade.

One interesting event took place while the *McRae* was awaiting her chance to run the blockade. In mid-September word reached Lieutenant Huger that Spain had given its official recognition to the Confederacy. The crew was overjoyed at hearing this. Not only did this mean international aide and recognition, it also meant that all Spanish ports, particularly in Cuba, could be used as safe areas for prizes to be brought. The prize money promised to each sailor would be handed out much more quickly than if otherwise. The crew celebrated for a time, but before long word reached the *McRae* that the news of Spanish recognition had been premature. Spain, just like France, had not yet given its recognition after all.

The *McRae* spent her time around the two forts in early October, continuing to wait for a breach in the Union blockade to make its escape. While waiting, Third Assistant Engineer Dent wrote to his father that "our engines are in tolerably good order that I am really afraid we wont [Sic.] run fast enough as she appears to be rather a slow coach. Our boilers are slam and I think consume too much steam."[67] By this time, Secretary Mallory had become determined to send his dispatches to England by another ship. The *McRae* would remain in the river, waiting for a chance to break the blockade and raid Union commerce. However, the crew spent

---

[65]   Ibid.

[66]   "Arrival of the French Corvette *Lavoisier*," *Richmond Daily Dispatch*, October 2, 1861.

[67]   "Letter from John H. Dent, Jr. to John H. Dent", 14 September 1861, *John Horry Dent, Jr., Letters*, University Libraries Division of Special Collections, The University of Alabama.

most of their time fighting mosquitoes instead of Union ships. One sailor serving by Forts Jackson and Saint Philip commented that "our duty consisted in watching out for the Yankees, and fighting mosquitoes – the largest I ever saw or felt."[68] Another sailor wrote "Mosquitoes almost eat us up down this low, they actually bite us through our clothes."[69] A Union marine that also spent some time in this area noted that "it is quite amusing to watch the different persons scattered around the decks, first striking themselves on one spot and then on another, and scratching here and there with a vigor."[70] The executive officer of the *Sumter*, Lieutenant John Kell also noticed the insects, commenting that "our crew had been so tormented with the heat and mosquitoes in the river below New Orleans that they begged to go to sea."[71] Though the sailors did not know at the time, the mosquitoes were the main cause of the constant yellow fever outbreaks that plagued southern Louisiana.

By October 5, Huger was becoming convinced that he would be unable to pass the Union blockade. He reported to the people of New Orleans that, as of October 2, several Union ships "are lying at anchor a short distance above the Head of the Passes."[72] Union warships patrolled the several passes of the Mississippi River that fed into the Gulf of Mexico. Huger ordered most of the rigging of *McRae* to be removed from the masts because it would not be used if the ship ended up as a gunboat patrolling the river.

---

[68] James H. Tomb, *Engineer in Gray: Memoirs of Chief Engineer James H. Tomb*, ed. R. Thomas Campbell (Jefferson, NC: McFarland and Company, 2005), 14.

[69] "Letter from John H. Dent, Jr. to John H. Dent", 4 Septembers 1861, *John Horry Dent, Jr., Letters*, University Libraries Division of Special Collections, The University of Alabama.

[70] "A Yankee Note Book," Galveston Tri-Weekly News, September 28, 1862.; Gusley, 38.

[71] John M. Kell, *Recollections of a Naval Life: Including the Cruises of the Confederate States Steamers, "Sumter" and "Alabama"* (Washington, DC: Neale Co, 1900), 148.

[72] "Increase of the Federal Force in the Mississippi," *New Orleans Bulletin*, October 3, 1861.

Commodore George N. Hollins

On October 9 a small squadron of makeshift ships joined the *McRae* at Fort Jackson. In command was Commodore George N. Hollins of Maryland. Hollins was a veteran of the War of 1812, having served on the *USS President* where he was captured. He also served in the Mexican War and was quite aggressive despite his age, having been born in 1799. After forty-seven years of naval service, he had been dismissed from the United States Navy in June of 1861 after he attempted to resign his commission. His entry into the Confederate Navy was in the Chesapeake Bay, where he took a small ship and boarded several Union merchants, capturing them for the Confederacy and bringing them to Fredericksburg, Virginia. He was then sent to the Gulf of Mexico to operate, finally being sent to command ships on the Mississippi River. The new squadron commander was determined to immediately strike at the Union ships blockading the mouth of the Mississippi River before the Union ships could consolidate their gains and establish a base in the Head of the Passes.

CSS Manassas

Sitting alongside Fort Jackson was a new privateer that had been outfitted with iron plating and with a ram. On October 11, the *McRae* anchored alongside the privateer, formerly known as the *Enoch Train*. Hollins initially requested of her owners that the *Enoch Train* be turned over to him. The reply was that commodore "did not have men enough to take her."[73] Hollins then had ordered Lieutenant Huger to seize the ram for government use. Huger ordered the crew to quarters and Lieutenant Alexander Warley took a boat to the privateer. Accompanying Warley in the boat was young Midshipman James Morgan. Morgan later wrote that "we found her crew lined up on the turtleback, swearing that they would kill the first man who attempted to board her."[74] When Warley boarded, the crew fled overboard, leaving the Confederate Navy in control of the vessel. Warley was detached from the *McRae* to take command of the newly christened *CSS Manassas*, which would later be purchased by the Navy Department for $100,000. The *Manassas* was the former *Enoch Train* bought by a local merchant and river captain, John Stevenson. Stevenson was a politically connected river captain who served as the secretary of the New Orleans Pilots Benevolent Society. Beginning on May 12, 1861, Stevenson began raising subscriptions from the best of the city to convert the ship into his proposed privateer by covering her in an inch of iron

[73]   Morgan, 55.
[74]   Ibid.

plating and fitting her with a ram. The *Enoch Train* was a prize herself of the privateer *Ivy*. After having his ship seized, Stevenson swore he would never again work with the Confederate Naval authorities. The *Manassas* was often described as resembling the shape of a cigar as "her hull projected only two feet above the water, and her plated top was convex causing cannon shot to glance off harmlessly."[75] Her largest drawback was the single 32-pounder that was permanently fixed forward. Being unable to traverse, the entire ship had to be moved to properly aim the gun at the enemy.

Now that Hollins had his ironclad ram, he intended to make a show of force. Reasons for why Hollins insisted on attacking the Union blockaders are mixed and unclear. Some sources claim that he was insistent on clearing the Head of the Passes of Union ships. Others claim that he wanted to test out the strength of the newly seized *Manassas*. Charles Read, onboard the *McRae*, believed that the entire attack was being launched to finally give the *McRae* a chance to clear the blockade into the open ocean which would follow the *Sumter's* actions and prey on Union shipping. One likely thought in Hollins' head was to strike against Union incursions on the river. The Head of the Passes remained unoccupied by Union warships until October 10. He likely wanted to strike at the blockaders before they could finalize and coordinate a defense at the Head of the Passes. Whatever the reasons, the Confederate squadron gathered at Fort Jackson and proceeded downriver to engage the enemy ships. One sailor wrote in a letter home that night that "we are going on a grand expedition tonight to attack Lincolns [Sic.] men-of-war now anchored at the Head of the Passes."[76] Around midnight of October 12, "the little fleet left the forts" steaming downriver.[77]

---

[75] Dictionary of American Naval Fighting Ships [DANFS] (Navy Department, Officer of the Chief of Naval Operations, Naval History Division), vol. 2, 546.

[76] "Letter from John H. Dent, Jr. to John H. Dent", 10 October 1861, *John Horry Dent, Jr., Letters*, University Libraries Division of Special Collections, The University of Alabama.

[77] "The Great Naval Victory," *New Orleans Daily Crescent*, October 14, 1861.

Battle of the Head of Passes

In the predawn hours of October 12, 1861 Hollins steamed his squadron south to the Head of the Passes. His forces consisted of the ironclad *Manassas*, mounting one gun and her ram; *McRae* and *Ivy*, four guns; *Jackson*, *Pickens*, and *Tuscarora*, two guns each; and *Calhoun*, five guns. The *Ivy* and *Calhoun* were both privateers that had recently been purchased by the Confederate Navy to bolster Hollins' forces. The ships departed their anchorages near Forts Jackson and Saint Philip at midnight. The Union squadron in the Head of the Passes consisted of the *USS Richmond*, twenty two guns; *USS Vincennes*, nineteen guns; *USS Preble*, ten guns; and *USS Water Witch*, four guns. The Union squadron was under the command of Captain John Pope, a career naval officer who had entered the United States Navy in 1816. The Union ships outgunned the Confederate squadron by a factor of over two to one, but several of Hollins' ships were armed with guns of a greater range than their Union opponents.

USS Richmond

It seemed that Captain Pope was not prepared to face Confederate forces. He left no boats upriver to serve as pickets or scouts. At 3:00 am, the *Manassas* rammed *USS Richmond* and sent a signal rocket into the air. The *Richmond*, however, was spared from most of the effects of the ramming because a coaling barge, the *Joseph H. Toone*, was made up alongside to resupply her. The *Manassas* rammed a hole into the *Richmond*, but most of the power was spent breaking the *Toone* and the *Richmond* away from each other. The strike did make, "a hole five inches in diameter in her hull."[78] During inspections of the *Richmond* after the battle, it was noticed that "she was struck a little abaft of the fore chains" and "a small indentation in her copper is visible; her great injury being below the water-line."[79] The rocket that was fired was the signal for the *McRae, Ivy,* and *Tuscarora* to release fire rafts filled with pitch, tar, and burning wood towards the Union squadron. These fire rafts were "braced apart from each other by timbers and secured together by a chain cable."[80] The *Jackson* and *Pickens* helped to guide the rafts downriver while the rest of the ships opened fire with their guns, creating panic amongst the Union ships. One sailor onboard the *Jackson* commented about the fire raft they released, writing that it "went

78   "Washington, Oct. 25," *Gallipolis Journal*, October 21, 1861.

79   "The Battle of the Passes: The Enemy's Account," *New Orleans Daily Picayune*, October 15, 1861.

80   "Particulars of the Naval Combat at the Head of the Passes," *Shreveport Daily News*, October 18, 1861.

down the river all in a blaze, and made a most magnificent sight to us, who were behind her, but to the Yankees it must have been the reverse.[81]

CSS Calhoun depicted after her capture by the Union Navy.
Commodore Hollins' flagship at the Head of Passes

Hollins' plan of overwhelming the Union ships into confusion worked. Third Assistant Engineer Dent wrote that "it was a terrible shock the *Bull Run* [*Manassas*] gave them."[82] The *Preble* saw the fire rafts and, in such a haste to get underway to avoid them, broke her capstan and had to cut her anchor chain loose to escape. Captain Pope ordered his ships to retreat to the Southwest Pass and at dawn, the four Union ships were seen retreating. In the confusion of the night engagement, Hollins believed he had forced all of the Union ships "aground on the Southwest bar, except for the sloop-of-war *Preble*, which I sunk."[83] However, the case was very different. The two larger ships, *Richmond* and *Vincennes*, ran aground at the bar, unable to escape while the *Water Witch* and *Preble* continued their retreat from the fire rafts, which had drifted to the western bank of the river harmlessly. The Confederate squadron gave chase and fired upon the two grounded ships. The Union guns had a smaller range than those of Hollins' ships,

---

[81]   Tomb, 24.

[82]   "Letter from John H. Dent, Jr. to John H. Dent", 15 October 1861, *John Horry Dent, Jr., Letters*, University Libraries Division of Special Collections, The University of Alabama.

[83]   "Gallant Attack on the Blockaders," *New Orleans Daily Picayune*, October 13, 1861.

and as was reported in New Orleans "the *McRae*, *Ivy* and *Tuscarora* led our fleet, and were the boats that kept up the fire on the retreating vessels."[84]

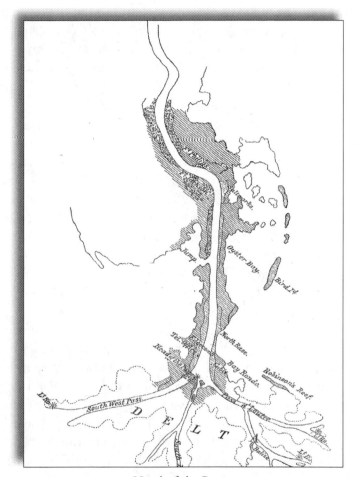

Head of the Passes

While steaming downriver, Master Read spotted the *Manassas* on the riverbank, noting that she had "run into a ship; had entangled her propellers, disabled her engines, and carried away her smokestacks."[85] Midshipman Morgan commented that the *McRae*'s gunners "opened fire with our nine-inch pivot gun on the *Richmond*, but from a very respectable

---

[84] "Particulars of the Naval Combat at the Head of the Passes," *Shreveport Daily News*, October 18, 1861.

[85] Read, 335.

distance."[86] The Union ships responded with their guns that could be traversed and aimed at the Confederate ships; being grounded meant that the ships could not maneuver their guns to bear on the enemy. The *Richmond*, which was grounded broadside in the river, returned fire on the *McRae* with most if her guns, but most of the shells fell short doing no damage. Engineer Dent "was on the Quarter and Engine Deck the whole time" and commented that "it was a beautiful sight to see" the Union ships in disarray.[87] Colonel Johnson Duncan in Fort Jackson sent a telegram to General David Twiggs in New Orleans that even at 9:00 am, "the broadsides are almost incessant."[88]

As the firing continued, the crew of the *USS Vincennes* was then seen abandoning the vessel; the captain had ordered the ship's magazine blown up to prevent the ship from falling into Confederate hands. Commander Robert Handy, in command of the *Vincennes*, mistook Captain Pope's order to retreat as an order to abandon his ship. With only two serviceable guns because Handy "hove overboard the rest of her armament, with her chains, anchors, etc., to lighten her" the *Vincennes* continued to fight even as she was being evacuated.[89] To add to the scene, Pope did not realize that the *Vincennes* was abandoned until her Commander Handy boarded the *Richmond* with his ship's American flag tied around his waist. Pope was furious and embarrassed. Fortunately for the Union sailors, the fuse that was lit was of poor quality and the ship did not explode. After a while, the Union sailors once again boarded the *Vincennes* and worked to refloat her.

Commodore Hollins, who had been onboard the *Calhoun* throughout the fight, now ordered his ships to withdraw upriver to the two forts. The Union ships were still much more powerful than his, and he had achieved victory through surprise. Hollins did not want to risk his ships in a full stand up fight. Besides, Hollins believed he had achieved his objective of forcing the Union squadron to abandon the Head of the Passes. Master Read noted that Lieutenant Huger was about to proceed past the Union ships to sea "to take advantage of what was regarded as the object of the

---

[86] Morgan, 57.

[87] "Letter from John H. Dent, Jr. to John H. Dent", 27 October 1861, *John Horry Dent, Jr., Letters*, University Libraries Division of Special Collections, The University of Alabama.

[88] "A Naval Brush with the Enemy at the Head of the Passes," *New Orleans Daily Picayune*, October 12, 1861.

[89] "The Attack on Our Squadron at the Mouth of the Mississippi," *Harper's Weekly*, November 9, 1861.

expedition, when the *McRae* was ordered to follow the other boats up the river to the forts."[90] On the way back upriver, the Confederate squadron had captured and towed upriver the *Joseph H. Toone* filled with fifteen tons of coal, which had been coaling the *Richmond*. She was abandoned in the hasty retreat of the Union squadron. Also, a supply of wood, which was ashore and being used to build a fort to hold the Head of the Passes, was burned. By 10:00, the battle was over.

Altogether, the Confederate squadron had won a small victory, mostly due to confusion and poor decisions by Captain Pope and his subordinates. Hollins' squadron had driven the Union Navy out of the Head of the Passes in a most embarrassing fashion and had captured a sizable amount of enemy supplies. Hollins labeled the battle a great victory, but as Union newspapers noted, the "report of a 'complete success,' is manifestly untrue."[91] The blockading force was not broken and Union ships instead simply placed themselves once again at each navigable pass that could lead into and out of the Mississippi River. Little damage was done to either force. Lieutenant Huger reported no casualties in the battle and that his gunners had fired a total of twenty-three shells at the *USS Richmond*, which had a shell burst in the captain's cabin and another destroy a small boat that was stored onboard. The *McRae*, however, was not allowed to escape the Mississippi River to the Gulf of Mexico and the Union blockade remained in place, though less coordinated than it would have been if conducted in the Head of the Passes. After the battle, Captain Pope was relieved. Also removed was Flag Officer William McKean, in command of the entire Gulf Blockading Squadron. Captain Pope's actions were described as "Pope's Run" in many newspapers. Even Gideon Welles, the Union Secretary of the Navy, felt the situation was most embarrassing.

The *McRae* was sighted below the forts at 12:30 that afternoon. Within an hour, two more Confederate ships were sighted; one was towing the captured *Joseph H. Toone*. Upon arriving at Forts Jackson and Saint Philip, Hollins telegraphed initial success to New Orleans and dispatched Midshipman James Morgan to travel immediately upriver bearing dispatches about the battle for Richmond. Rumors of the battle began to reach New Orleans at around noon on October 13 and by 3:00 that afternoon, "glorious news had been received that the expedition had

---

90   Read, 336.
91   "Thingamajigs," *White Cloud Kansas Chief,* October 31 1861.

been entirely successful."[92] Another paper wrote that "henceforth the name of Hollins will be mentioned with pride throughout the broad extent of the Southern Confederacy."[93] The Louisiana legislature voted a unanimous resolution of thanks. One sailor onboard commented that "all on the *McRae* thought we would go down[river] the following night, but great was our disappointment when we found that we were neither to attack the enemy again nor attempt to go to sea."[94]

The *McRae* made its way back to New Orleans, "arriv[ing] at her anchorage opposite the city at eleven o'clock" on the morning of October 15.[95] She then proceeded to refill her coal supply and make still more repairs to her engine and propeller shaft. Once again the *McRae's* inadequate engine was causing her considerable trouble. Lieutenant Huger, denied before by Hollins to move past the blockade, completed work on his engine and steamed the *McRae* downriver to get his ship ready to make a run past the scattered Union blockade and prey on enemy commerce. However, many in the Union believed that the *McRae* had escaped the blockade following Hollins' victory. It was printed in New York that "the privateer *McRae*, commanded by Lieut. HUGER, late of the United States Navy, has probably gone to the Mediterranean."[96]

The *McRae* would spend twelve days docked at New Orleans making repairs. The ship left the city on October 26, 1861 and anchored at the Quarantine station about five miles upriver from Forts Jackson and Saint Philip. However, while at Quarantine, there was a severe outbreak of fever onboard, and the ship had to return to New Orleans to receive medical care. On November 3, Third Assistant Engineer Dent wrote home that "we have a great deal of sickness on our ship. We have at this moment 45 invalids."[97] It was at this time that Hollins determined to prevent the *McRae* from running the blockade because it had become too risky; the blockaders off New Orleans had captured two Confederate supply ships

---

92 "Naval Triumph in the Passes," *New Orleans Daily Picayune*, October 13, 1861.

93 "The Great Naval Victory," *New Orleans Daily Crescent*, October 14, 1861.

94 Read, 336.

95 "Return of the *McRae*," *The Daily True Delta*, October 15, 1861.

96 "Apprehended Attack on New-Orleans: Archbishop Purcell on the War. The Reported Death of Ben McCulloch. The Search for the Sumter from the Washington Star. A Novel Breastwork. War Items,." *New York Times*, October 11, 1861.

97 "Letter from John H. Dent, Jr. to John H. Dent", 3 November 1861, *John Horry Dent, Jr., Letters*, University Libraries Division of Special Collections, The University of Alabama.

in October and another three in November. Not wanting to risk the capture of his gunboats, Hollins instead ordered the *McRae* to serve as his flagship for his small Mississippi River squadron. Originally purchased and outfitted to hunt Union commerce, the *McRae* would now serve as a traditional river gunboat defending the Mississippi. The *McRae's* mission to England would have to be completed by another ship. The *CSS Nashville* left Charleston, South Carolina in late October for England, carrying dispatches and naval officers to man ship being built in Europe. She became the first ship of the Confederacy to enter a European port.

The *McRae* arrived at New Orleans on November 3, and Lieutenant Huger immediately offloaded many of his officers and crew for recovery. Records indicate the crew was divided and sent to wherever there was space in hospitals. Sailors were sent to Charity Hospital, the Marine Hospital, and to the *CSS Saint Philip*, a hospital ship lying off of the city, to receive treatment. Day after day more of the crew was admitted for severe cases of fever. Those who reported to hospitals on November 3 alone were Fireman First Class Thomas Henry from Ireland, Fireman First Class James McDonald from Scotland, Boatswain's Mate Thomas Wilson, Ordinary Seaman Bernard Allen from Louisiana, Second Class Fireman John Campion from Ireland, and Ordinary Seaman Thomas Murtha from England. At least twenty-seven of the *McRae's* sailors were admitted to New Orleans hospitals in November and December of 1861. Less serious cases were allowed to remain on the *McRae* to receive treatment. Even Lieutenant Huger would be struck with the fever, having to recover in the arms of his fiancée ashore. In early January, 1862, Doctor Lynch travelled to Charleston, South Carolina to marry his fiancée, so it is likely that most of the illness onboard the ship was over by then.

At this time, the Confederate government decided to reassign many of the officers onboard. The limited experience they had fighting at Ship Island and at the Head of the Passes meant that the officers were some of the most experienced sailors in the Confederacy. In addition, so many senior officers were no longer needed since the *McRae* was no longer bound for England. The ship was billeted with a larger number of officers than typical because many were supposed to remain in England to man ships being built under contract by Commander James Bulloch.

Midshipman James Morgan, after spreading word of the victory at the Head of the Passes, received a furlough to visit his home in Baton Rouge. He was present to witness the death of his father, who was ill. Upon his return, Morgan recalled that "with the exception of Captain Huger, Sailing Master Read ('Savez'), and Midshipman Blanc, all of the line officers, whom I loved so dearly, were detached."[98] Lieutenant Alexander Warley was permanently reassigned to command the ironclad *Manassas*. Transferred to assist Warley with maintaining the turtleback ironclad was Acting Master William Levine, a Louisianan by birth. Lieutenant John Dunnington was ordered to take command of the *CSS Pontchartrain* which had just completed its conversion from a riverboat in New Orleans. The *Pontchartrain* would serve on the upper defenses of the Mississippi River in Missouri, Tennessee, and Arkansas. Midshipman Sardine Stone was promoted to lieutenant and transferred to serve onboard the *CSS General Polk*, a vessel recently placed into commission to defend the upper portion of the Mississippi River. Midshipman John Comstock was also promoted to lieutenant and received orders to report onboard the *CSS Selma*, a gunboat in Mobile. Lieutenant John Eggleston and Midshipman Henry Marmaduke were ordered to Norfolk, Virginia to report onboard the famed ironclad *CSS Virginia*.

Master Charles "Savez" Read also received a promotion to lieutenant and assumed the duties as the executive officer in place of Warley. Chief Engineer Virginius Freeman was reassigned to the Charleston, South Carolina Naval Station; Second Assistant Engineer Charles Levy received orders to report to Charleston, South Carolina and would eventually end up onboard the *CSS Tallahassee*, and Third Assistant Engineer William Jackson would be transferred to the ironclad *Arkansas* under construction at Memphis, Tennessee. Second Assistant Engineer Samuel Brock took charge of the engineering department onboard the *McRae*. Assisting Brock were Second Assistant Engineer Henry Fagan, who was appointed from Washington D.C., Third Assistant Engineer John Dent of Alabama, and Third Assistant Engineer Charles Jordan of Virginia. To supplement the loss of engineers, Third Assistant Engineer James H. Tomb, who was appointed from Florida, transferred onboard in early February from his position onboard the *CSS Jackson*. Tomb had completed his studies and was appointed as a third assistant engineer in the United States Navy in May of 1861. He declined the position and instead joined the Confederate Navy. Assigned to assist Surgeon Arthur Lynch was Assistant Surgeon Marcellus Christian from Virginia and Surgeon's Steward Owen McGrath. Both assistants had prior service in the United States Navy before the war.

---

[98]   Morgan, 60-61.

Two senior line officers also reported onboard in early 1862. Lieutenant Thomas Arnold of Arkansas was a former midshipman in the United States Navy who had resigned from the service in 1855. Lieutenant Thomas Fister [sometimes spelled Pfister], a Pennsylvanian by birth, was a member of the Confederate States Revenue Service who had voluntarily rendered his services to Lieutenant Huger. He had previously served in the United States Revenue Service, precursor to the Coast Guard. Lieutenant Fister remained officially assigned to the Confederate Revenue Cutter *Pickens* while temporarily assigned onboard the *McRae*.

While the ship was at New Orleans letting its sailors recover from their illnesses, Read and the rest of the crew were preparing the ship for service as a Mississippi River gunboat. Once again, the *McRae* underwent conversions. The large spars atop the masts were fully removed, the sails were unbent and stowed, the rigging was removed, and the masts were partially disassembled; the *McRae* would now solely rely on steam propulsion instead of both steam and sails. Fresh line was brought onboard, the engine and boilers were inspected and fully repaired, the men were drilled more often, and a state of readiness was raised. Engineer Dent wrote home about the overhaul, stating to his father that "this work will make her run with more ease than she did before."[99] Huger and Read made attempts to arm the *McRae* with more guns of larger caliber, but they were unable to procure any. The crew must not have liked the overhaul because it meant long hours of additional work tacked on the day's normal routine, but Lieutenant Huger felt it necessary to ensure that the ship was in a ready state to give battle.

Newly promoted Lieutenant Read, just twenty one years old, remained in charge of the *McRae* while Lieutenant Huger recovered from his fever ashore. The crew regularly received liberty in New Orleans during this time if they were not sick and the day's work was completed. On one occasion many crewmembers returned to the *McRae* drunk and several sailors made demands to be let ashore to acquire more alcohol. Lieutenant Warley had been a strict disciplinarian and many onboard believed that Read would not be as tough. Lieutenant Read surprised everyone when he ordered Midshipman Morgan to shoot the first man attempting to leave the ship. Later that night, the crew managed to smuggle more alcohol onboard and the level of intoxication grew amongst the enlisted sailors. "Savez" Read

---

[99]   "Letter from John H. Dent, Jr. to John H. Dent", 7 January 1862, *John Horry Dent, Jr., Letters*, University Libraries Division of Special Collections, The University of Alabama.

immediately roused the entire crew on deck. Read then ordered the crew to climb what remained of the masts and rigging, keeping them aloft throughout the night, threatening to shoot the first man who came down. Not one drunk sailor came down all night. At dawn, he let the crew down and the ship went about its normal daily routine. Neither the crew nor Read ever brought up the incident again, but many of the sailors developed a new sense of respect for their twenty one year old executive officer.

Not all sailors enjoyed this treatment by Lieutenant Read. Seaman John Bates deserted from the ship on November 18. Two days later, Seaman William Newman and Ordinary Seaman Thomas Brown also deserted. They were not alone. In February 1862, Fireman First Class James Robenson and Landsman George Smith both deserted. Both however, were caught in New Orleans and returned to the *McRae*. Besides desertion, several sailors were arrested in New Orleans for various reasons and returned to the *McRae*. Steward Francis Hamilton and Ordinary Seaman James Welch were arrested on 30 January 1862. Fireman Second Class George Gibbs was arrested on 17 February.

Shortly After the incident involving the intoxicated crew, Huger returned to duty with the other sailors in hospitals who had recovered from their illnesses. Commodore Hollins also formally came onboard and flew his pennant from the *McRae*. Midshipman Morgan was assigned to be his aide-de-camp. The *McRae* remained in the area for a month, spending her time between New Orleans and patrolling the Head of the Passes. Third Assistant Engineer Dent wrote home that "I think Capt. Huger is trying for sea orders again," but nothing came of the attempt.[100] Hollins was determined to use the *McRae* on the river.

---

[100]   Ibid.

CHAPTER FIVE

The Upper Mississippi

I N Saint Louis, Missouri and Cairo, Illinois, Union forces were amassing a large waterborne force of ironclads. The civil engineer and Indiana native, James B. Eads, was responsible for the initial building of ironclads in Missouri and Illinois. Their missions were to, in cooperation with ground forces, drive down the internal waterways of the Confederacy and seize control of the Mississippi River. It was a common held belief among the Confederate high command that, as President Jefferson Davis noted, "The greatest danger to New Orleans was from above, not from below the city."[101] Fortifications had been constructed at Columbus, Kentucky; Island Number Ten on the Mississippi River; New Madrid, Missouri; and Fort Pillow, Tennessee to block Union ships from moving down the Mississippi River. In January 1862, Stephen Mallory ordered Hollins, seen as a hero now for fending off the Union blockade of the Mississippi River, to bring his ships upriver to assist in the defenses of Kentucky, Missouri, and Tennessee. Hollins forces were ordered to provide naval support for these strategically located river positions.

The positions on the Mississippi River were only the left flank of the Confederate position in Kentucky and Tennessee. Positions were held across the two states in a wide arc stretching from the Mississippi River to Fort Henry on the Tennessee River and Fort Donelson on the Cumberland River. The line then continued east to Bowling Green, Kentucky, pushing on to the Cumberland Gap. This entire theatre was under the direction of General Albert Sydney Johnston, a graduate of the West Point Class of 1862 and a career army officer that many believed was the most capable

---

[101]   Davis, 207.

army officer in the country. In addition, he was a personal friend of President Jefferson Davis.

Commodore Hollins and Lieutenant Huger left New Orleans by rail travelling to Columbus, Kentucky to ascertain the situation and make preparations for the Confederate ships. This left Lieutenant Read in charge to take the *McRae* upriver. Before the *McRae* steamed north, several members of the crew in hospitals at New Orleans were discharged from the navy for illnesses; these were the most severe cases left from the fever that had struck the crew. Those discharged from the navy included Private Newman Trowbridge, a marine that was from Louisiana, Seaman Richard Andrews, Seaman James Parker from England, Seaman Ed Jones of Maryland, and Ship's Boy John Sidney of Louisiana. Seaman James Myers, however, died in the hospital on Christmas Day 1861 due to complications from pleurisy. Those deemed fit for service were quickly returned to the *McRae* before she began her trek north.

Before heading upriver, the *McRae's* crew learned of a major event that could change the war itself. By Christmas of 1861, the men onboard had learned about the *Trent* Affair, where the Union gunboat *San Jacinto* boarded the British mail steamer *Trent* and captured two Confederate diplomats on their way to Europe. The officers of the *McRae* knew that this act violated international law. Third Assistant Engineer Dent wrote to his father that "This Mason and Slidell affair has caused a good deal of excitement and speculation."[102] A prospective alliance with the naval juggernaut of England heartened the crew for a while. However, it amounted to nothing when, in early 1862, the diplomats were released on the threat of England declaring war.

Most of the warships around New Orleans joined the *McRae* upriver. There has been great speculation about which ships were sent upriver at what times. It is known that the *McRae* was alongside the docks of New Orleans as late as January 22, 1862, as Third Assistant Engineer John Dent wrote to his father on that day. Three sailors that were in hospitals ashore were discharged from the navy on February 8, 1862. Third Assistant Engineer James Tomb wrote that he was transferred from the *CSS Jackson* to the *McRae* on February 4, 1862. It is likely that the *McRae* began her journey upriver sometime around February 8. The *CSS Tuscarora*

---

[102] "Letter from John H. Dent, Jr. to John H. Dent", 23 December 1861, *John Horry Dent, Jr., Letters*, University Libraries Division of Special Collections, The University of Alabama.

is known to have made the journey upriver in November 1861 and it is believe that the floating battery *New Orleans* did not move upriver until March 1862. The *Jackson* was reported upriver in November 1861, one engineer commenting that she was "an old tug boat carrying two guns."[103] The *General Polk* was operating in the upper parts of the river as early as December 1861. The *CSS Livingston* was operating in the northern part of the river in January 1862. At a court of inquiry held 1863, Commodore Hollins testified that he "left New Orleans in January or February, 1862" for Columbus.[104] It is likely that Lieutenant Read made the journey upriver accompanied by the *CSS Ivy*, and possibly the *CSS Pontchartrain*. These were all recently converted gunboats and the *Ivy* had the distinction of being a former privateer that had captured two Union merchant ships in 1861.

Due to the current of the river and the poor conditions of her overused engine, the *McRae* made poor time on its travels, occasionally "bumping into a mud bank and lying helpless."[105] The small squadron made stops at Baton Rouge and Vicksburg, Mississippi where citizens lined the riverbanks and cheered as the ships would stop briefly for supplies and news before moving on. This was the first time the people of Vicksburg had a chance to see ships of the Confederate Navy. To them, the small flotilla must have seemed imposing.

The journey upriver, however, was not easy or routine. While steaming upriver just below Vicksburg, the *McRae* managed to run aground in a foggy night on the bank of the plantation of Jefferson Davis. Midshipman Morgan commented that "for this heroic performance, it is needless to say, none of us were promoted, and we lay ingloriously stuck in the mud until we were pulled off by a towboat."[106] Other ships fended even worse while making the trek. While moving upriver on November 23, 1861, the *CSS Tuscarora* caught fire and sunk off of the city of Helena, Arkansas.

Newspapers speculated the reasons behind Hollins' movement. The *Nashville Union and American* commented that Hollins' ships and Johnston's army would unite to force "military movements on a grand

---

[103] "Letter from John H. Dent, Jr. to John H. Dent", 26 November 1861, *John Horry Dent, Jr., Letters*, University Libraries Division of Special Collections, The University of Alabama.

[104] *Official Records of the War of the Rebellion* [OR] (Washington, D.C.: Government Printing Office, 1884 – 1927), ser. 2, vol 2, 76.

[105] Morgan, 62.

[106] Ibid.

scale, involving great strategy and important battle."[107] Union papers also documented the move, though slightly prematurely with his personal presence in the area, commenting that "The doughty Capt. Hollins had gone up the river with his fleet."[108] Further columns in Union papers noted that "extensive excitement prevails ... relative to the threatened attack on Columbus [by Union ironclads]" and that "Hollins had gone there with his fleet."[109] The sailors onboard the *McRae* did not expect an offensive. Instead they would "expect an attack at Columbus hourly" by the Union forces based at Cairo.[110]

The *McRae* managed to arrive at Columbus without any further excitement and anchored alongside the rest of what had become known as "Hollins' fleet". This fleet however was not nearly as prepared for combat as they may have appeared to the crowds that gathered and cheered them on at Baton Rouge, Vicksburg, and Memphis. None of the Confederate ships had been gunboats before the war except for the *McRae*, which was the only ship with proper halyards and signal lamps. Hollins was forced to rely on "a rough little steam launch, about twenty-five feet in length" under the direction of Midshipman James Morgan to convey orders to the other ships in the squadron or to convey instructions on land to army commanders.[111] The lack of proper signal equipment demonstrates how improvised the Confederate Navy had to be while taking on the might of the United States Navy. The Union forces opposite Columbus, however, were not aware of the deficiencies of Hollins' forces. Several Union deserters that were captured by the Confederates reported that "the Federals are more apprehensive of an attack from us than we from them, owing to our preparations in this place, and the sudden appearance of Commodore Hollins' fleet."[112] The Confederate sailors also believed this, writing that

[107] "Our Bowling Green Correspondence," *Nashville Union and American*, November 26, 1861.
[108] "The Latest War News," *Vermont Phoenix*, November 28, 1861.
[109] "New York, Nov. 25.," *Burlington Free Press*, November 29, 1861.
[110] "Letter from John H. Dent, Jr. to John H. Dent", November 26, 1861, *John Horry Dent, Jr., Letters*, University Libraries Division of Special Collections, The University of Alabama.
[111] Morgan, 65.
[112] "From Columbus" *The Athens Post*, December 20, 1861.

"Columbus can never be taken by bombarding it and Ft. Pillow below is equally as strong. They are natural fortifications."[113]

The *McRae*, along with the rest of "Hollins' Fleet," arrived upriver just in time. Union forces began a 350 mile wide offensive in early 1862 directed to push Confederate forces out of Kentucky and Tennessee. Forts Henry and Donelson fell to a combined Union army and navy force under the command of Major General Ulysses Grant and Flag Officer Andrew Foote. For a brief moment, forces trapped in Fort Donelson believed that "Commodore Hollins with the ram, *Manassas*, and thirteen Confederate Gun-boats passed Memphis ... on his way to our relief."[114] Hollins, however, held his forces in reserve and Fort Donelson surrendered unconditionally, giving the United States Army its first major victory of the war. The fall of Forts Henry and Donelson made holding Columbus untenable and forced its evacuation, along with General Johnston's main headquarters at Bowling Green, Kentucky. Most Confederate forces retreated into Tennessee. Hollins' gunboats withdrew from Columbus, moving to protect Island Number Ten and New Madrid, the next defensible position on the Mississippi River. While anchored off of New Madrid, Midshipman Morgan witnessed the arrival of General Jeff Thompson with his partisans. They were scouting Union forces advancing from Columbus. Morgan wrote that General Thompson yelled to Hollins onboard the *McRae* that "There are a hundred thousand Yankees after me and they have captured one of my guns, and if you don't get out of this pretty quick they will be on board of your old steamboat in less than fifteen minutes!"[115] Thompson was exaggerating about the numbers, but Union troops were definitely advancing to New Madrid.

---

[113] "Letter from John H. Dent, Jr. to John H. Dent", 4 December 1861, *John Horry Dent, Jr., Letters*, University Libraries Division of Special Collections, The University of Alabama.

[114] "Fort Donelson, Feb. 13, 9P.M." *Clarksville Chronicle*, February 14, 1862.

[115] Morgan, 62-63.

Brigadier General M. Jeff Thompson, Missouri State Guard

Union forces were quick to follow. On March 3, 1862, the Union Army of the Mississippi, some twenty-five thousand strong, arrived in front of New Madrid and attempted to storm the town. They were led by Brigadier General John Pope, a West Point graduate and veteran of the Mexican War. Pope was attempting to outflank the Confederate positions at Island Number Ten without provoking a large-scale battle. "Hollins' fleet" responded by firing on the Union forces advancing against New Madrid. Two forts were in place on either side of New Madrid with rifle pits connecting the two around the town. The *McRae* joined the bombardment with its nine-inch Dahlgren pivot gun. Lieutenant Read would write that as the battle began, "I saw [Colonel Edward W.] Gant[t] when the Yankee shells first began to fall in our lines. He took the 'shell fever' quicker than any man I ever saw."[116]

Hollins' gunboats helped to stem the initial Union assault, forcing General Pope to lay siege to the entrenched Confederates. Engineer James Tomb noted that "Pope could have taken them [New Madrid] at

---

[116]   Read, 337.

any time had our ships been away."[117] Union forces agreed with Tomb's assessment. The *Baltimore Sun* printed of New Madrid that "the Federal officers believe that the place can easily be taken after the boats are driven off."[118] Additionally, the *Hartford Daily Courant* printed that "our officers are confident of an early and complete victory, if the enemy's gunboats are driven away."[119] The gunboats proceeded to harass the Union siege operations by firing upon and "annoy[ing] the enemy's working parties considerably."[120] General Pope agreed, commenting in his official report that "it would not have been difficult to carry the intrenchments [Sic.], but it would have been attended with heavy loss, and we should not have been able to hold the place half an hour exposed to the destructive fire of the [Confederate] gunboats."[121]

During the siege, it became difficult at times for the Confederate land and naval forces to communicate with each other. Hollins had to frequently send young Midshipman James Morgan ashore with messages to Brigadier General John P. McCown, in command of the defenses of New Madrid. On one such occasion, an army officer insulted Morgan, calling him a child who was too young to be in combat. Sixteen year old Morgan became infuriated and was preparing to challenge the insulting officer to a duel, which was illegal in the Confederate Navy. While discussing the matter, however, Morgan was soothed by Lieutenant Charles "Savez" Read, who commented that the insulting officer "was nothing but a damned soldier, and a volunteer at that."[122] Both Morgan and Read, like many regulars in the navy, looked down on the volunteer officers as temporary amateurs not doing a proper job, particularly in the army where commissions were easy to come by to those politically connected.

Days passed, and the siege operation continued as Union trenches edged slowly closer to the Confederate positions. Midshipman James Morgan later wrote that "the dirt commenced to fly while the artillery kept up a desultory fire."[123] Union forces launched another assault against the Confederate entrenchments on March 7. The Forty-Third Ohio and Sixty-Third Ohio Infantry Regiments, accompanied by the Eleventh

---

[117] Tomb, 28

[118] "The War News," *Baltimore Sun*, March 8, 1862.

[119] "Fighting at New Madrid, Missouri," *Hartford Daily Courant*, March 10, 1862.

[120] Read, 337.

[121] OR, ser. 1, vol 8, 81.

[122] Morgan, 64.

[123] Ibid.

Ohio Independent Light Artillery Battery broke through the Confederate entrenchments and advanced into New Madrid. An editor embedded with the Union troops reported that they advanced "until we were in possession of two of the streets of the town."[124]

Once into the town, he went on to note that "the gunboats then opened upon us with shells and for the space of half an hour the air over our heads was literally filled with them, bursting in all directions."[125]

Map of the Siege of New Madrid and Island Number Ten

From the *McRae's* quarterdeck, the crew observed the Eleventh Ohio Independent Light Artillery Battery, led by Captain Archibald D.A. Constable, advancing into New Madrid. Lieutenant Huger ordered the *McRae* to open fire with the nine-inch Dahlgren pivot gun. One shell

---

124   "From the 48D Regiment," *Belmont Chronicle*, March 20, 1862.
125   Ibid.

struck the front of the column of artillerymen, bursting in the center of the group. Sixteen year old Midshipman Morgan, who was standing alongside Commodore Hollins at the time, later wrote that "to see horses, men, and guns cavorting in the air was a most appalling sight."[126] The crew of the Dahlgren reloaded their cannon and continued the attack on the Union artillery. After several more shots, the gun exploded sending the "muzzle falling between the ship's side and the river-bank while half of the breach [Sic.] violently str[uck] the deck" between where Morgan and Hollins stood.[127] Fortunately, no one onboard was hurt in the incident. Hollins looked over to young Morgan and commented that "Youngster, you came near getting your toes mashed!"[128] The *McRae*, however, would never receive a replacement nine-inch pivot gun, despite the working of Commodore Hollins who "sent up for one of the guns of this battery [*CSS New Orleans*]" for replacement.[129] The guns could not be spared and no replacement gun was ever sent. The Union attack of March 7 was defeated thanks to Hollins' gunboats. Union trench lines, however, were now on the very outskirts of New Madrid threatening the stability of the entire Confederate position.

The siege of New Madrid continued. With Union trenches on the outskirts of New Madrid, buildings on the edge of town began to block fire from "Hollins' fleet." Hollins ordered Midshipman Morgan to move into the outskirts of New Madrid and set fire to several of these buildings. Morgan went ashore, leading a detail of sailors from the *McRae*. While they were scouting the buildings, the party found a large piano in working order, which they brought to the riverbank. They returned to the outskirts of town and began burning several barns, coming under fire of Union guns as they did so. Once Union artillery began to fire on them, the small detachment made a dash to the river. While running to his boat, Morgan, as he would later describe it, "felt a sting in the upper portion of my left arm."[130] The wound was caused by a spent bullet that caused no major damage. The detail returned onboard the *McRae* without any other casualties, with their mission accomplished, and with the piano.

Upon closer inspection, Lieutenant Charles Read discovered "a number of treasonable letters under the lid of the piano" and was convinced that

---

[126] Morgan, 65.
[127] Ibid.
[128] Ibid.
[129] "Western Military Correspondence," *New Orleans Daily Crescent*, March 24, 1862.
[130] Morgan, 68.

that whoever owned it had been providing intelligence to Union soldiers.[131] Several days later, two women boarded the *McRae* and demanded to see Lieutenant Huger wishing for their piano to be returned. Coincidentally, Lieutenant Read was standing officer of the deck when they came onboard, and he was determined to see to the women personally. Read warned the women that if the piano was truly theirs, then they would be subject to arrest for treason to the Confederacy. The women were flabbergasted "and both said it was not their property and they did not want it."[132] They left the *McRae* without the piano. Lieutenant Read never found out if the women were the actual owners of the piano or if they had been passing information to the Union Army.

At one point during the siege of New Madrid, General Pope advanced troops to Point Pleasant, ten miles downriver, in an attempt to cut off the Confederate positions from Memphis. One Memphis newspaper speculated that "Commodore Hollins was to have proceeded down with two gunboats … to break up the nest, which he doubtless succeeded in doing."[133] Hollins, however, refused to leave the banks of New Madrid lest General Pope succeed in storming the town.

While holding back the Union forces at New Madrid, the men of the engineering department onboard the *McRae* became angry with the chief engineer, Second Assistant Engineer Samuel Brock. Brock liked to spend his time on watch in the engine room reading books on naval regulations, using up the ships oil in lamps to light the engineering space at night. In response, Brock ordered that no engineering officer could read in the engine room to conserve the lamp oil. James Tomb described Brock as "a most disagreeable man, and most arbitrary."[134] The day after Brock forbade reading on watch, Fireman First Class George Kendricks returned onboard from a visit to the riverbank. At his side was a pig which he had killed and intended to let the crew feast upon. Lieutenant Thomas Fister, who was the officer of the deck at the time, let Kendricks onboard without comment.

Shortly after this, "the ordinary beat, followed by two rolls" that served as the general quarters alarm, indicating action with the enemy, was sounded.[135] The call was due to an expected enemy attack which failed to

---

[131]   Tomb, 28.

[132]   Ibid., 29.

[133]   "Point Pleasant," *Memphis Daily Appeal*, March 9, 1862.

[134]   Tomb, 29.

[135]   Confederate States of America Navy Department, 37.

materialize. While at quarters, Brock saw the pig tied down in front of a furnace so as to not be in the way. When Brock asked Fireman Kendricks about the pig, he commented that it belonged to the other engineering officers and the midshipmen. Brock became furious and ordered the pig to be thrown into the furnace and, as Tomb put it, "all the pork chops that the mess had been counting on for a few days went up in smoke and smell."[136] Kendricks lost his precious dinner but would not let Brock get the last punch in this contest. To add to Brock's dislike, he forbade reading in the engine room while on watch to conserve oil.

A couple of days later, Third Assistant Engineer James Tomb entered the engine room a few minutes before the forenoon watch began and noticed Brock sitting and reading. Brock placed the book in a desk and left the room after Tomb relieved him. Tomb immediately opened the desk and got the book. Calling over Fireman Kendricks, he asked who had violated Mr. Brock's orders about reading in the engine room. After Kendricks answered that he did not know, Tomb ordered the fireman to "put this book the way the pig went, and don't be long about it either, as I intend to carry out Mr. Brock's orders."[137] Kendricks and the other enlisted men in the engine room rushed to the furnace and threw the book in the fire, each with a smile on their faces. At approximately 8:30 that morning, Brock entered the engine room to reclaim the book, which he had borrowed from Lieutenant Fister. Tomb told the senior engineer what he had done, as per Brock's own orders. The senior engineer stormed out of the engine room, furious. The engineering department had won a small victory over their hated chief engineer, but Tomb felt that "it would have been for the good of the service, if Brock had followed the pig and the book."[138] The situation in the engineering department got so bad that several of the engineers onboard expressed their wishes to be transferred to other ships to get away from Brock. In the end, the engineers would win their struggle against Brock, who would be superseded in April, 1862 as the chief engineer by Second Assistant Engineer Henry Fagan.

Several days into the siege of New Madrid, the evening picket of the *McRae* landed ashore and captured two prisoners. Ship's Corporal John O'Neill held the men in custody after they were taken onboard for questioning. The two Union soldiers did not speak any passable English,

---

[136] Tomb, 29.
[137] Ibid., 30.
[138] Ibid.

and it was discovered that they were both German immigrants. Through a translator, Lieutenants Huger and Read learned that the two immigrants "had been landed one day and enlisted the next."[139] Engineer Tomb noted with disdain that the Union Army was using conscripts that had no part in the conflict to overpower the Confederate military forces. He did not take note, however, of the many Europeans currently serving onboard his own ship.

On March 13, 1862, heavy Union siege guns arrived in front of New Madrid and began to shell the Confederate positions. After ten days of being besieged, Commodore Hollins and Brigadier General John McCown decided to evacuate New Madrid that night. Around midnight, Hollins' squadron docked along the banks of the river to begin the on-load of men and supplies. Much equipment, however, had to be left behind due to time restraints. Lieutenant Charles Read noted that "it rained in torrents, and our poor soldiers, covered with mud and drenched with rain, crowded on our gunboats, leaving behind provisions, camp equipments and artillery."[140] Most of the soldiers ran onboard the gunboats without any sense of order and discipline. The small gunboat *Joy* was nearly capsized by the onrush of soldiers. Lieutenant Read was determined to not let the *McRae* be swamped in such a manner. He met the oncoming solders at the brow of the *McRae* and drew his sword demanding that the soldiers calm down and restore discipline. One large soldier, presenting himself as the leader of a pack of troops, challenged Read to let them onboard. Read then struck the man with the flat of his blade and ordered the soldiers to get into formation. The men then marched onboard without further incident. Once loaded with soldiers, the *McRae* cast off with the rest of "Hollins' fleet" and steamed downriver, abandoning New Madrid to Union forces and leaving Island Number Ten cut off from Confederate support.

---

[139]   Ibid, 31.
[140]   Read, 337.

Docks of New Madrid, Missouri. Shown after the occupation by Union forces.

The next morning, Union siege guns were about to open fire when they discovered the abandoned Confederate positions. Union reporters noted that "The rebels evacuated both forts last night, crossing the river by means of transports during a heavy storm. They left fourteen heavy guns, a large quantity of ammunition, tents, camp equipage, several flags, about three hundred horses and mules, besides wagons, stores, [and] officers' baggage."[141] General Pope, however, noted to General Henry Halleck that the captures were even greater and included "twenty-five pieces of heavy artillery ... two batteries of field artillery; an immense quantity of fixed ammunition; several thousand small arms; hundreds of boxes of musket-cartridges; three hundred mules and horses; [and] tents for an army of 12,000 men."[142] Confederate reports in Memphis were far more conservative, commenting that "everything was saved except the large guns."[143]

The squadron anchored the morning of March 14 several miles downriver at Tiptonville, Tennessee and offloaded the soldiers that crowded the gunboats. Hollins' fleet had evacuated five regiments of infantry and three companies of artillery without incident. The army forces marched from Tiptonville and made it to the riverbank opposite Island Number Ten, where they were then brought to the island to assist in its defense.

---

141 "Important News from New Madrid: The Town in the Hands of Our Troops" *Gallipolis Journal*, March 20, 1862.

142 "St. Louis, March 15," *Gallipolis Journal*, March 20, 1862.

143 "Telegraphic," *The Semi-Weekly Shreveport News*, March 21, 1862.

The ships remained at anchor for several days covering the troops as they prepared new fortifications and made preparations to move. While at anchor one morning, Commodore Hollins sighted some men working near a stockpile of wood on the western side of the river. Just as he determined to send the *McRae's* steam launch to find out what the men were doing, they revealed several fieldpieces which began to open fire upon the Confederate gunboats. The gunboats returned fire at the Union ambushers, and during the exchange of shots, a yawl boat was cut from the *CSS Maurepas* by a shell and drifted downriver. The *McRae* then "ceased firing, and went a mile below to pick up the boat" as the rest of the squadron silenced the Union guns one by one.[144] It was reported in Memphis that "the Federals attempted to plant a battery opposite this landing [at Tiptonville], but were deterred by the timely interference of Commodore Hollins, who drove them away and took their guns."[145]

Hollins then signaled from the *McRae* for the squadron to steam several miles downriver out of range of that Union gun position should enemy forces move to occupy it again. The same action was repeated the next day as the same Union gunners moved their cannon to meet the Confederate gunboats again. This time, Hollins withdrew his ships under the protection of the guns of Fort Pillow. On March 15, Hollins wrote to Beauregard that the *Manassas*, which was en-route to joining the flotilla, was ordered back to New Orleans. The commodore commented, however, that due to "some injury received from a 'snag' I fear she will be detained some days in Memphis to repair."[146]

Though seen as an act of cowardice by many army soldiers, Hollins actions were well perceived as the Union gunners had their position protected by earthen fortifications while the gunboats were exposed on the open river. In addition, "Hollins's fleet" was short of ammunition and, as he wrote to General Pierre G.T. Beauregard, he did not "wish to throw it [ammunition] away without some return from the enemy for it."[147] The lack of ammunition was not limited to Hollins' ships in Tennessee. The Commodore wrote to ships in Louisiana waters that "The scarcity of ammunition at the present time is very great," and captains should "reserve

144   Read., 338.
145   "Tiptonville," *The Semi-Weekly Shreveport News*, March 28, 1862.
146   ORN, ser. 1, vol 22, 738.
147   Ibid.

your shots for when the enemy's vessel should be within the full range of your guns."[148]

Since New Madrid had fallen to Pope's forces, Island Number Ten was now cut off. W.J. Tenney, a prominent contemporary encyclopedia editor, wrote in 1866 that "by possession of these works Gen. Pope commanded the river so as to cut off all communication from Island No. 10 from below." [149] Hollins was now compelled to send a ship each night past enemy gun positions at New Madrid to bring supplies to the entrenchments and to remove the wounded on the island. During these passages, the ships were subject to bombardment by Union artillery and by rifles from ashore. Third Assistant Engineer Dent described the results of these runs, writing home that "our boats have a great many [musket] balls through them."[150]

On the night of April 4, the *USS Carondelet* steamed past the Confederate batteries on Island Number Ten and linked up with Pope's forces at New Madrid. Lieutenant Read wrote that the *Carondelet* "attacked in detail our small batteries which had been constructed to prevent the crossing of troops" from New Madrid to Tiptonville to further isolate Island Number Ten.[151] One night soon after, the *Carondelet* was seen moving Union infantry across the river and General McCown sent a message to Hollins urging him to attack. Hollins declined, noting that the *Carondelet* "was iron-clad, and his fleet were all wooden boats, he did not think he could successfully combat her."[152]

[148] ORN, ser. 1, vol 17, 165.

[149] W.J. Tenney, *The Military and naval History of the Rebellion in the United States* (New York: Appleton & Co, 1866), 163.

[150] Letter from John H. Dent, Jr. to John H. Dent", 23 March 1862, *John Horry Dent, Jr., Letters*, University Libraries Division of Special Collections, The University of Alabama.

[151] Read, 338.

[152] Ibid.

USS Carondelet

One interesting event took place on the river when Hollins ordered Midshipman Morganto take the *McRae's* steam launch, with two sailors as a crew, and investigate the riverbank upriver for Union gun batteries. Hollins carefully ordered Morgan to not round the point in the river, which was where the *Carondelet* was located. Morgan determined there were no Union gun position on the bank and then rounded the river, encountering the *Carondelet*. The Union ship began to give chase to Morgan's launch, which rapidly retreated downriver to the Confederate squadron. As Morgan withdrew, a Union battery began to fire on him. The steam launch returned to the *McRae*, but in his haste, overloaded the little steam engine on the launch. The engineer onboard had tied down the safety to allow the launch to escape the *Carondelet*. When Samuel Brock noticed this from the deck of the *McRae*, he shouted to Morgan "For God's sake, don't stop, sir; she will blow up!"[153] Hearing this, Morgan steamed away from the *McRae* and yelled out to Hollins, "*Tom Benton* coming down, sir!"[154] The *USS Tom Benton* was the largest Union ironclad in the area and all Union ironclads in the area were referred to as *Benton* at the time. After releasing the safety and allowing steam pressure to bleed to normal levels, Morgan came alongside and boarded the *McRae* and gave his formal report to Hollins of the *Carondelet*. Hollins asked Morgan why he had rounded the point in the river and when the young midshipman

---

[153] Morgan, 66.

[154] Ibid.

explained to Hollins that he thought it was safe, Hollins erupted, yelling that "You dared to think, sir! I will have you understand that I am the only man in this fleet who is allowed to think!"[155] In the end, no damage was inflicted on Hollins' ships as they made their midnight runs with supplies. The confederate squadron would remain at Fort Pillow or Tiptonville making their midnight runs through April 8, 1862 when Island Number Ten surrendered to the encircling Union forces. Hollins then moved his squadron permanently to Fort Pillow, the next defensive position on the river. When the *McRae* arrived at Fort Pillow, Hollins directed Midshipman Morgan ashore. He reported the fall of Island Number Ten to Brigadier General John B. Villepigue, in command of the fort. Morgan later wrote that he also advised General Villepigue "to prepare for an attack by the enemy's ironclads."[156] As the army surrendered on Island Number Ten, the floating battery *New Orleans* was scuttled. At least one sailor, Lieutenant George W. Gift of Tennessee, made his escape from the island and found himself serving onboard the *McRae*.

Commodore William C. Whittle

While anchored at Fort Pillow, droves of refugees passed the *McRae* moving south towards Memphis to escape the Union invaders. One day while anchored at the fort, Lieutenant Read, along with Third Assistant

---

155   Ibid., 67.
156   Ibid., 71.

Engineers John Dent and James Tomb, went ashore in one of the *McRae's* small boats. While ashore, they encountered a woman who had evacuated her home and took some two hundred bales of cotton with her. The woman had no way to get the cotton to safety in Memphis and she instead asked the men to burn the cotton to keep it out of Union hands. Read offered to buy the cotton on behalf of the Confederate Navy, providing her with a receipt for it. He then systematically burned every bale. The woman in turn offered the officers several jars of preserves and four large turkeys as thanks. The wardroom became the center of attraction for the officers for several days as they feasted on the provided food. Tomb commented that the worst part of the affair was that "Brock, being in the ward room, would also get his share of the booty."[157] Tomb did manage, however, to hide the jam preserves from the hated engineering officer, which continued to outcast Brock from the rest of the engineering department.

Flag Officer David Farragut

On April 9, news reached Commodore Hollins that would change everything for the *McRae* and her crew. A message had arrived from Commodore William C. Whittle at New Orleans asking for immediate assistance. Flag Officer David Farragut's Western Gulf Blockading

---

[157] Tomb, 34.

Squadron was advancing upriver from the Gulf of Mexico and was threatening to capture the city. Any help that could be sent to New Orleans was vital, and Hollins delayed none, immediately sending a message to Secretary Mallory requesting permission to bring his squadron downriver.

Commodore Hollins believed that his gunboats would stand a better chance of defeating Farragut's ships, which were exclusively wooden gunboats, instead of fighting the several Union ironclads patrolling the upper portions of the river. Also, Hollins knew that New Orleans was vital to the Confederacy, and its loss could very well mean the loss of the war. Mallory, however, held a different opinion and ordered Hollins and his ships to stay where they were. Mallory believed that the ironclads *CSS Louisiana* and *CSS Mississippi*, which were nearing completion at the New Orleans shipyards, would be able to defeat Farragut's force and then move upriver and help destroy the enemy ironclads there. However, Mallory's beliefs about the Confederate ironclads were not fully informed; the *Louisiana* was indeed near completion, but the *Mississippi* still had at least another full month of work before even hoping to be ready for battle.

Flag Officer Farragut's squadron entering the Mississippi River

Hollins determined to take matters into his own hand. The very day he received the news, the Commodore and young Midshipman Morgan departed the *McRae* and began to steam downriver for New Orleans onboard the faster gunboat *Ivy*, not even waiting for Secretary Mallory's response to his telegram. On their way downriver, Midshipman Morgan spent a brief time at his family's home in Baton Rouge while the *Ivy* received dispatches and coal. After reaching New Orleans, Hollins made headquarters in the Saint Charles Hotel and sent young Morgan down to Fort Jackson to begin coordination between the naval forces and the fort's commander. When he arrived, Union naval forces had already begun bombarding the forts and Morgan, accompanied by Lieutenant Beverly Kennon, moved to Fort Jackson. As they approached the fort, "a shell fell into the moat and gave us a dirty shower bath, at the same time disturbing several large alligators who lashed the water furiously with their tails."[158] After conferring with army commanders, he returned upriver to New Orleans to report to Hollins and continue naval preparations.

Hollins left Lieutenant Huger in charge of the squadron until Commodore Robert Pinckney arrived from Memphis, Tennessee, where he was currently on leave. Upon Pinckney's arrival, Huger was to turn over command of the squadron to him and then take the *McRae* downriver as fast as possible. The day after Hollins left, Lieutenant Huger took the squadron upriver to scout out the enemy ironclads. No enemy ships were discovered until "just after dark our attention was attracted by someone on shore, hailing and waiving a torch" who informed Huger that the Union ironclads were anchored just a couple of miles upriver.[159] The next morning, Huger sent the gunboat *Pontchartrain*, still led by the *McRae's* own Lieutenant John Dunnington, to attempt to draw out one of the enemy ships. However, the entire Union squadron was soon steaming downriver in chase of the *Pontchartrain* and Huger, upon seeing seven enemy ironclads, determined to withdraw immediately to the protection of the guns at Fort Pillow. Upon reaching that position, the Union ironclads began shelling the fort, to no avail, and after Confederate batteries returned fire, withdrew that night.

Commodore Pinckney soon arrived at Fort Pillow, and Huger, obeying Hollins' orders, proceeded to take the *McRae* downriver. While on their way downriver, Tomb noted that "as we passed Memphis, we saw no signs of guns being mounted on the bluff, but at Vicksburg there was apparently active work going on above the hills."[160] Union forces in Tennessee were reporting as late as 24 April that lying Confederate forces amounted to

---

[158]   Morgan, 71.
[159]   Read, 339.
[160]   Tomb, 24.

"fourteen gunboats and the ram *Manassas* lying off the forts, and that Captains Hollins and *McRae* were also there."[161]

Arriving at New Orleans on April 15, Huger dispatched Lieutenant Read ashore to report to Hollins at his headquarters at the Saint Charles Hotel while the ship refilled its coal bunkers. Read found Hollins anxious to engage the enemy ships, and the commodore informed Read that he intended "to attack the enemy's fleet of wooden ships below the forts and drive them out of the river."[162] Read, along with Midshipman Morgan who Hollins ordered back onboard, returned to the *McRae* informing Huger of the Commodore's intentions. However, just hours after their meeting, Hollins received a dispatch from Secretary Mallory relieving him of his command and ordering him immediately to report to Richmond to explain his actions in disobeying orders instructing him to remain in Tennessee. The Commodore that everyone believed could defend the river better than anyone else would not be taking part in the most important battle on the Mississippi River in the war. Hollins turned over command of all naval forces in the area to Commodore William Whittle, who immediately dispatched Commander John K. Mitchell to take command of all naval forces assembling at Forts Jackson and Saint Philip. Before steaming downriver, Huger left Midshipman James Morgan ashore as he suddenly came about with a severe illness. Morgan was allowed to stay at his brother's residence in New Orleans to recover. The *McRae* then steamed downriver, arriving at the forts on April 16, "at anchor in the stream, near the shore, and about [three-hundred] yards above Fort St. Philip."[163]

---

[161] "The Situation," *New York Herald*, April 24, 1862.
[162] Read, 341.
[163] ORN, ser. 1, vol 18, 332.

Defending New Orleans

T HE CITIZENS OF NEW ORLEANS believed that the city was prepared to meet the approaching Union forces. Lieutenant John Wilkinson, a naval officer serving in the city, commented that "the citizens were under the impression that the place was impregnable."[164] The military strength in the city itself, however, was weaker than advertised. In February 1862, Louisiana Governor Thomas Moore was instructed to send six regiments north to join General Albert S. Johnston's forces in Kentucky. They were meant to augment the losses of Confederate Army forces lost in surrender at Fort Donelson. These six regiments would later participate in the Battle of Shiloh while the *McRae* was supporting the garrison at Island Number Ten. In early April, an additional three-thousand state troops from the New Orleans area were dispatched to Tennessee, to offset casualties from the Battle of Shiloh. The men sent north were completely armed and equipped by the state of Louisiana. Also sent north were over one million rounds of ammunition and enough gunpowder for five thousand men, all made in foundries and powder works in New Orleans, as well as thousands of rifles.

To make up for the loss of manpower in the area, New Orleans Mayor John Monroe activated some ten-thousand men of the state militia. These were mostly immigrants who were, at the time, exempt from Confederate service but who had volunteered to defend the New Orleans area in an emergency. General Mansfield Lovell, in command of the defenses of New Orleans, wanted the militia to maintain positions along the Mississippi

---

[164]   John Wilkinson, *The Narrative of a Blockade Runner* (New York: Sheldon & Co, 1877), 13.

River near the site of General Andrew Jackson's victory against the British in the War of 1812. In addition, they maintained army supply and training camps spread throughout the city and government buildings within the city limits. The militia, however, was not as well equipped as the men sent north to Tennessee. Joining the militia was another two to three-thousand men of the Confederate Provisional Army that had not been transferred north to Tennessee. When the time came, however, the militia would, for the most part, choose to not fight and instead abandoned their positions, possibly saving New Orleans from a street fight that could have destroyed the city, such as what would happen later in the war to Fredericksburg, Virginia; Vicksburg, Mississippi; Atlanta, Georgia; and Richmond, Virginia.

Major General Mansfield Lovell

New Orleans had many defensive positions surrounding the city. To protect against attacks from upriver, Confederate authorities constructed Fort John Morgan and created a barrier that could block ships several miles upriver from the city. These defenses were built where present day Causeway Boulevard in Metairie, Louisiana is located. The powder magazine of Fort John Morgan can still be visited today. South of the city was the Chalmette battery, constructed on the spot where General Andrew Jackson had defeated the British in 1815. Across the river from Chalmette was the McGehee battery providing additional support. In the outlying areas were Forts Pike, Macomb, and Livingston which protected coastal Louisiana and the entrance to Lake Pontchartrain north of New Orleans.

Brigadier General Johnson Duncan

The main defenses that the people of New Orleans relied upon, however, were Forts Jackson and Saint Philip. Fort Saint Philip had been in service since the War of 1812. In 1814, it had defeated a British fleet moving upriver to attack New Orleans, forcing British soldiers to advance against General Andrew Jackson at Chalmette. Fort Jackson had been built after the war to bolster the defense of the Mississippi River. Fort Jackson had room for ninety-seven heavy cannon while Fort Saint Philip could mount fifty-two guns. Brigadier General Johnson Duncan was in overall command of the army forces at the two forts. Commanding Fort Jackson was Lieutenant Colonel Edward Higgins who was part of the amphibious operation to Ship Island in 1861. The forts were manned by one-thousand Louisiana regular soldiers. Among the garrisons of the two forts were nine companies of Louisiana heavy artillery, two companies of Louisiana infantry, and a full company of men from the first battalion of the Confederate Regular Army, and civilian volunteers from New Orleans. Harper's Weekly reported that Fort Jackson "had cost the United States nearly a million of dollars" to construct while in the case of Fort Saint

Philip "the Government paid for its construction two hundred and four thousand dollars."[165]

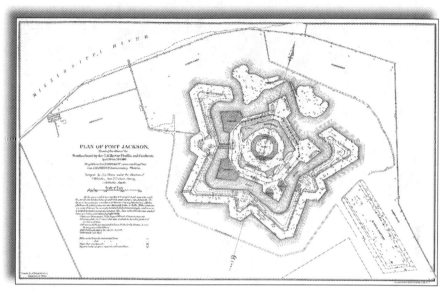

Fort Jackson

The military had also constructed a second barrier across the river made up of "schooners anchored across the river, in line abreast, between the forts, and chains and lines were passed from vessel to vessel."[166]

This would prevent any enemy ship from coming upriver without getting tangled in the obstruction and under the guns of the forts. Union forces were aware of the chain obstruction. One Union naval officer later wrote that it was formidable "because of the swift current down and the slowness of the ships below, which together, would prevent them from striking it a blow of sufficient power to break through."[167]

---

[165] "New Orleans," *Harper's Weekly*, May 10, 1862.

[166] Read, 341.

[167] Alfred Thayer Mahan, *The Gulf and Inland Waters* (New York: Charles Scribner's Sons, 1883), 70-71.

Deck of US Mortar Schooner

Farragut's plan was simple. He would advance his squadron up the Mississippi River and anchor it just below the forts. Commander David D. Porter would then besiege the two Confederate forts with a flotilla of mortar schooners. These schooners were "of from 200 to 300 tons each, of great strength and solidity, and carrying each a mortar, weighing 8 ½ tons, of thirty-nine inches length of bore, forty-three inches external and fifteen inches internal diameter, and intended to throw a 15-inch shell weighing, when unfilled, 212 lbs."[168] Porter's plan was to force the forts to surrender within forty-eight hours of beginning the bombardment. Once the forts surrendered, Farragut would steam upriver and land Major General Benjamin Butler's army of twelve-thousand soldiers in the city. Farragut would then continue steaming upriver in an effort to unite with the Union squadron that had just captured Island Number Ten led by Flag Officer Andrew Foote.

---

[168]   Tenney, 191.

Commander David Dixon Porter

The struggle for New Orleans was a battle for time. Under construction in the Crescent City were two of the most powerful ironclad warships ever conceived. The *Louisiana*, built by E.C. Murray of New Orleans, had two paddlewheels and two screw propellers. Railroad iron covered her casemate in two layers. When Union forces began their approach up the Mississippi River, the unfinished *Louisiana* was towed downriver and moored near Fort Saint Philip. Work continued on her through the bombardment and two river unarmed steamboats had been sent with the *Louisiana* "for the accommodation of the mechanics who were still at work on board."[169]

---

[169] Wilkinson, 15.

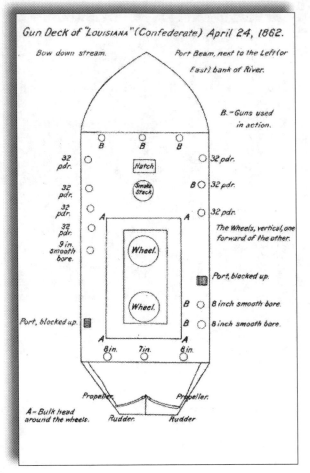

Diagram of the *CSS Louisiana*

The *Mississippi*, under the care of the brothers Nelson and Asa Tift, was designed to be the most powerful ironclad built by either side during the war. She was to feature three screw propellers capable of propelling her up to fourteen knots. Designed for twenty guns and to be fitted with up to three and three- quarters inches of iron plating in places, she would be more formidable than the famed ironclad *Virginia*. These two ironclads were being built with great expectations. They were designed to clear the Mississippi River of Union forces and break the blockade at the mouth of the river. Construction was delayed, however, by many factors. Lack of building materials, shipyards, iron, and guns were just the beginning. Worker strikes and the drawing of skilled labor into the army also added delays. President Davis was aware of the lack of facilities, commenting that, to build the two ironclads, "they had to prepare a shipyard, procure lumber from a distance, have the foundries and rolling-mills adapted to such iron work as could be done in the city."[170] The *Mississippi* was months away from being complete by April of 1862 but the *Louisiana* was very near completion, just needing her engines to be fully installed and her guns mounted. Every day Union forces were delayed was another day closer to the *Louisiana* being fully capable and able to sweep Union ships out of the river. If the forts could hold Farragut's ships at bay until she was completed, then the Union ships might also delay their attack long enough for the *Mississippi* to be finished.

Commander John K. Mitchell

Joining the garrisons of Forts Jackson and Saint Philip were several ships. Commander John Mitchell had at his disposal: the *CSS Jackson*, under Lieutenant F.B. Renshaw and mounting two thirty-two pounder cannon; the *CSS McRae*; the ironclad ram *CSS Manassas*, still under the command of Lieutenant Warley and mounting one gun; the unfinished ironclad *CSS Louisiana*, led by Commander Charles F. McIntosh and mounting sixteen guns of which eight were in a position to be used against Union forces while she was anchored; and a pair of steam launches armed with one howitzer each that served as scouting ships. The *Louisiana* still did

---

[170]   Davis, 209.

not have her engines fully installed and would operate as a floating battery in the coming fight until they were made ready. Joining this force were two gunboats operated by the Louisiana State Navy that agreed to serve under Mitchell's command, the *Governor Moore*, under Lieutenant Beverly Kennon, and the *General Quitman*, under Captain Alexander Grant. Each Louisiana ship was armed with two thirty-two pounders. Six ships of the River Defense Fleet, organized earlier in 1862, were also present. One naval officer described these ships as having their engineering equipment "protected by heavy timber barricades, filled in with compressed cotton; and they were prepared with bar-iron casting around their bows to act as 'Rams'"[171] Each ship had been confiscated by the Confederate Army and outfitted with one or two guns each for the defense of the river. In fact, Lieutenant Huger accompanied the confiscation detachments to help inspect the ships to help prepare them better. Eight ships had already been sent upriver to help defend Memphis, Tennessee. Their leader was none other than Captain John Stevenson. Stevenson's memory had not faded regarding when Lieutenant Alexander Warley had seized the *Manassas*, and he had no intentions of taking orders from the Confederate Navy.

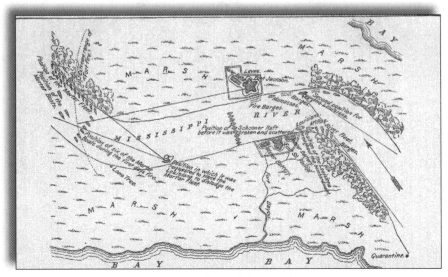

Position of Confederate Ships

Commander Mitchell also had charge of a number of fire rafts. These unmanned rafts were piled with tar, oil, and wood. A handful of tugs

---

[171]   Wilkinson, 14.

and tenders would guide these burning rafts into approaching Union ships in the hope of creating a panic and spreading fire from ship to ship. Altogether, there were some twenty-one ships, most improvised gunboats armed with less than the *McRae*, at anchor near the forts to help defend New Orleans. These defenses made the people of New Orleans believe that their city was impregnable. Even in Virginia, Confederate leaders thought these defenses were enough to hold the city. General Robert E. Lee, in a letter to his wife dated April 22, 1862, wrote that "The news from N[ew] Orleans is encouraging. It is reported but not confirmed that the forts below the city still hold out, that two of the enemy's boats are sunk & that the *Louisiana* (iron clad) went down last night to the assistance of the forts."[172] The transfer of trained troops out of state, ill-supplied state militia, constant delays on the two ironclads, and a lack of a unified naval command structure, however, would soon play havoc on the people of New Orleans.

Mortar Schooner Firing on Fort Jackson

---

[172] Letter from Robert E. Lee to His Wife, *The Wartime Papers of Robert E. Lee* (Boston: Little, Brown and Co), 154.

When Huger anchored the *McRae* by Fort Saint Philip on April 16, 1862, a bombardment of Fort Jackson by Union mortar ships was already underway. Huger immediately ordered a part of his crew to go assist the *CSS Louisiana*, which was continuing "labors upon the machinery and battery" to prepare for battle.[173] The *McRae's* crew continued to provide support for the *Louisiana*, which was full of engineers, carpenters, and mechanics from New Orleans attempting to have her fully completed before the Union ships decided to fight. As the crew continued to help prepare the *Louisiana*, it also provided fire support to the forts for a short time. The shells fired, however, landed short and Lieutenant Colonel Higgins in Fort Jackson soon sent a note to Huger to cease firing and conserve ammunition and powder for when Union ships were closer. Captain William Robertson, in command of the water-battery in Fort Jackson, noted that the support by the *McRae* was the only action taken by the Confederate Navy "to render us any assistance, until they were forced into action by Farragut's advance."[174]

On April 22, Lieutenant Huger was ordered to take his engineers and survey the unarmed tugs *Belle Algrine* and *Mosher*, which had been bringing supplies to the forts when they collided with each other. In a report to Commander Mitchell, Lieutenant Huger and Second Assistant Engineer Samuel Brock commented that the *Belle Algrine* "leaks badly in the bows, from two holes knocked in her," while the *Mosher* "loosened the after-bearing of her shaft."[175] Brock further wrote that "I trust by to-night both vessels will be serviceable" and both tugs were fully repaired by the next day.[176]

---

[173] Wilkinson, 16.

[174] William B. Robertson, "The Water-Battery at Fort Jackson," *Battles and Leaders of the Civil War Vol. 2: The Struggle Intensifies*, (New York: The Century Co, 1887), 100.

[175] OR, ser. 1, vol 6, 538.

[176] Ibid.

CSS Louisiana

Against the improvised Confederate squadron, Flag Officer Farragut had brought some twenty-four gunboats, seventeen mortar schooners, and seven support ships. His goal was to silence the forts and Confederate naval forces, clearing the way for the liberation of New Orleans. Major General Benjamin Butler, in command of twelve-thousand New England soldiers, was prepared to fight in, capture, and occupy the city. Altogether, there were some sixty-nine ships on both sides anchored in the vicinity of Forts Jackson and Saint Philip. The largest ship-to-ship naval battle of the Civil War was set to begin.

The bombardment of the forts continued nonstop through April 23. Late in the night of Easter Sunday, April 20, Captain Henry Bell led the *USS Itasca* and the *USS Pinola* upriver. The two ships landed small parties on one of the sunken hulks in the river and, while under fire from Fort Jackson, created a gap in the chain barrier large enough for Farragut's ships to pass through. By Easter Sunday, both sides had sustained significant damage. Some fifteen guns had been disabled in Fort Jackson while the mortar schooner *USS Maria J. Carlton* had sunk when she received a direct hit from a Confederate shell. Several other Union ships had also received damage. The damage to Fort Jackson, however, was quickly repaired each night, with the exception of the barracks which had caught on fire. In addition, several breaches had been made in the levee around Fort Jackson and parts of the parade grounds were flooded.

For Farragut, it was becoming a real question of time. Every day the *CSS Louisiana* came closer to being completed. Once operational, it would be likely that she would be able to delay Farragut's advance long enough for the *Mississippi* to be finished. With both ironclads operational, Farragut would be easily defeated by the Confederate naval forces. Farragut decided to act now and became determined to take some of his ships and make a run past the forts and Confederate ships in the hope of taking New Orleans and forcing the surrender of the remaining forces downriver.

On the afternoon of April 23, Lieutenant "Savez" Read paid a visit to Fort Jackson. Read and Lieutenant Colonel Higgins observed the Union ships arranging themselves in lines while smaller boats were placing markers in the river to designate avenues of advance. Read later wrote that after seeing this, "we were both of the opinion that a move would be made on the forts the following night."[177] Read then returned to the *McRae* and prepared the ship for the upcoming battle. He described his preparations, writing that "I directed the cable to be got ready for slipping and a man stationed to unshackle it at a moment's warning; one-half of the men to be on deck; steam to be up; the guns cast loose and loaded with 5-section [second] shell."[178] Read was not the only naval officer to believe a Union attack was imminent. Lieutenant John Wilkinson, executive officer of the *CSS Louisiana*, wrote that "the naval officers were quite sure that an attempt would soon be made ... to force the passage."[179]

While Read was visiting Fort Jackson, Lieutenant Alexander Warley of the *Manassas* took a moment to come onboard his old ship and pay a visit to Lieutenant Huger. Warley was dropping off letters that should be delivered to his family if he were to die in the coming battle. Ironically, Lieutenant Warley found Huger just about to call on him for the same purpose. The two men spoke for a while and Warley later wrote that "judging from the character of the officers in the enemy's fleet, most of whom we knew — [we] believed the attack was at hand."[180] Preparations for the imminent battle continued into the night, and most of the *McRae's* crew, as well as the rest of the Confederate forces, got little sleep.

Flag Officer Farragut had prepared to take a large portion of his available ships and make a dash past the forts and Confederate squadron. Sixteen

---

[177] Read, 342.

[178] Ibid.

[179] Wilkinson, 16.

[180] A.F. Warley, "The Ram *Manassas* at the Passage of the New Orleans Forts," *Battles and Leaders of the Civil War Vol. 2: The Struggle Intensifies* (New York: The Century Co, 1887), 89.

ships divided into three divisions would attempt to pass the Confederates. The first division of seven ships was led by Captain Theodorus Bailey, a career officer with forty-four years of service including command of the *USS Lexington* during the Mexican War. The second division of three ships was under the direction of Farragut himself. The third division of six ships was under the command of Captain Henry Bell, a thirty-eight year veteran of the navy including command of the *USS San Jacinto*. The ships involved with the passage were strengthened when anchor cables were "stopped up and down on the sides in the line of the engines."[181] In addition, "each commander made his own arrangements for stopping the shot from penetrating the boilers or machinery that might come in forward or abaft, by hammocks, coal, bags of ashes, bags of sand, clothes bags, and in fact every device imaginable."[182] Commander David Porter's mortar schooners would provide covering fire during the passage and continue to bombard the forts after Farragut had moved upriver to New Orleans. Several gunboats would remain with Porter to protect the mortar schooners from a waterborne attack. Meanwhile, General Butler's infantry would land and move through the swamps in an attempt to get into the rear and cut supply lines for Fort Jackson and Fort Saint Philip and, if need be, to assault them. It was a risky plan which would divide Union naval strength in the area and leave part of it isolated, but Farragut believed that it would work.

[181]   Tenney, 194.
[182]   Ibid.

Battle of Forts Jackson and Saint Philip

At 3:35 am on April 24, 1862, Fort Jackson opened fire on the advancing Union ships. Porter's mortars immediately returned fire. The officer of the deck ran and awoke Lieutenants Huger and Read who immediately gave the alarm to go to quarters. Meanwhile, Quartermaster Thomas Rohman informed Third Assistant Engineer James Tomb, who was on watch in the engine room, that Union ships were approaching. Tomb prepared the engine for full operation and, by 3:40, reported that "all hands [were] at quarters and 15 pounds of steam" pressure was built up in the *McRae's* boilers.[183] Union ships were fast approaching the Confederates, and Huger ordered his guns to open fire. The first shots were let loose before the ship had even weighed anchor. To raise the anchor, the *McRae* had to gain headway with its engine to remove strain from its anchor and chain. While the *McRae* was weighing anchor, the engine overheated and had to be stopped to cool, leaving the ship at anchor for several more minutes. While waiting for the engine to cool, the *USS Hartford* and the *USS Mississippi* steamed past. Huger opened fire on them even while at anchor. Once the engine was cool enough, Huger weighed the anchor and began to move the *McRae* across to the other side of the river to block passage of the Union ships. After firing ten rounds, the twenty-four pound rifled

---

[183]   ORN, ser. 1, vol 18, 345.

pivot gun exploded, leaving the *McRae* with only her six broadside guns to bear on the enemy.

The Union ships were taking fire almost immediately. An officer onboard the *USS Cayuga*, the first ship to pass the forts, commented that "The captain of one of my guns is struck full in the face by a solid shot and his head is severed from his body; as he falls the lockstring [Sic.] in his hand is pulled and the gun is discharged!"[184] The Union officer rushed to the gun to inspect the damage, leaving a junior officer in his place when "a shell explodes and tears his [the junior officer's] right arm away!"[185]

USS Brooklyn

By 3:50 the *McRae* was steaming for the western bank of the river. As each ship began to open fire, it added its cannon shots to the din. Onboard the *McRae*, the noise was so terrific that the engineers "could not hear the bell or gong at times" to indicate speed changes.[186] Attempting to engage an enemy gunboat, Huger ordered the ship to turn to port slightly, however just as he gave the order "two large, full-rigged ships were discovered a short distance astern, one on each quarter, coming rapidly up"[187] The two ships nearly collided with the *McRae*, but the engineers cut off steam pressure

---

184   Frederick Stanhope Hill, *Twenty Years at Sea* (Riverside Press, 1893), 176.
185   Ibid.
186   Tomb, 38.
187   ORN, ser. 1, vol 18, 332.

to the engine, and they barely missed colliding. James Tomb later wrote this was because the "engine became hot, due to the injector choking."[188] Huger immediately gave the order to prepare to repel boarders by shouting verbally and "springing the rattles and sounding the gong together."[189] Most of the crew then came to the weather-deck to repel boarding parties. Sailors armed with swords and cutlasses would be arranged in a line with a second line of men armed with pikes formed behind them. A third line, consisting of marines armed with muskets and bayonets would provide fire support to sweep the decks of the enemy. However, no Union boarding parties would come.

USS Iroquois

The two Union ships, the *USS Brooklyn* and the *USS Iroquois*, mistook the *McRae* as a friend. The *Brooklyn* was a large ship, carrying twenty-one cannon and displacing 2,500 tons. The *Iroquois* displaced 1,000 tons and mounted four guns. She was similar to the *McRae* in many respects and the two ships were formidable and equal opponents. Captain Thomas Craven, commanding officer of the *Brooklyn*, believed that the *McRae* was a Union ship and gave the order to hold fire. Commander John Barlett onboard the *Brooklyn* believed that the *McRae* was a Confederate ship, and he yelled to Craven that "It can't be the *Iroquois*! It is not one of our vessels, for her smoke-stack is abaft her mainmast!"[190] Barlett, in the end, obeyed Captain Craven's order not to fire. This was despite that fact that Barlett had his

---

188   Tomb, 38.

189   Confederate States of America Navy Department, 38.

190   John Russell Barlett, "The Brooklyn at the Passage of the Forts", *Battles and Leaders of the Civil War Vol. 2: The Struggle Intensifies* (New York: The Century Co, 1887), 67.

hand on the lanyard of one of his guns, and "the gun had been depressed, and a 9-inch shell would have gone through her [the *McRae's*] deck and out below the water-line."[191]

Captain Thomas Craven, Commanding Officer of the *USS Brooklyn*

After the two Union ships passed, Huger moved the *McRae* so that the starboard guns could fire upon one of them. His target was the *USS Iroquois*. First the starboard battery opened fire, and then Huger quickly turned the *McRae* around and presented the port battery, sweeping the deck with grape-shot inflicting even more damage. It was around this time that the twenty-four pound pivot gun burst. Men in Fort Jackson noticed the damage that the *McRae* was inflicting. Lieutenant Colonel Higgins wrote in his report that "I observed the *McRae* gallantly fighting at terrible odds-contending at close quarters with two of the enemy's powerful ships."[192]

The *Iroquois* responded to the *McRae's* broadsides with several shots from her six cannon. One eleven-inch shell slammed into the sail room starting a fire. A second shell "exploded in the smoke stack just above the flames and filled the fire room with fire and ashes from the furnaces. At the same time an eleven inch shell passed through the fire room wounding

---

[191] Ibid.
[192] OR, ser. 1, vol 6, 548.

a number of men by splinters."[193] The shell had enough force to smash through the other side of the hull landing in the river, but not before mortally wounding First Class Fireman George Kendricks by ripping off part of his head.

Huger dispatched "Savez" Read and a detail of men to deal with the blaze, which if allowed to spread, could explode the magazine and kill everyone onboard. This threat was very real as the magazine was separated by the sail room with a thin pine bulkhead of two-inch thickness. While Read dealt with the fire, Huger moved the *McRae* towards the riverbank in case he had to order the crew to abandon ship. Read remembered explicit orders from Huger to inform him "when the fire should reach the shell locker bulkhead."[194] The fire detachment met with Acting Midshipman Samuel Blanc, who was in charge of the powder division and the ship's magazine and Carpenter's Mate P.G. Newman who, as the chief carpenter onboard, was in charge of the *McRae's* "force and channel pumps,

the fire-engine, the division tubs, and, in short, all the supply of water in case of fire."[195] Read and his damage control party managed to extinguish the blaze after several tense minutes of damage control efforts.

CSS Manassas engaging *USS Brooklyn*

[193] "Letter from Charles W. Read to John H. Dent", 28 April 1862, *John Horry Dent, Jr., Letters*, University Libraries Division of Special Collections, The University of Alabama.

[194] ORN, ser. 1, vol 18, 332.

[195] Confederate States of America Navy Department, 12.

While Read was dealing with the fire, the fight with the *Iroquois* continued. By the time the blaze below decks was contained, several other Union ships were now targeting the *McRae*. It appeared that the ship would be overwhelmed when suddenly the *CSS Manassas*, commanded by the *McRae's* own Lieutenant Alexander Warley, arrived. The *Manassas* advanced against the Union ships in an attempt to ram one, but "as soon as they discovered her they started up the river" away from the *McRae*.[196] The *Manassas* continued to give chase. As the *Iroquois* began to steam upriver away from the *McRae*, she fired one last round of canister. The canister slammed into the smokestack and quarterdeck of the *McRae* and, as Lieutenant Read later wrote, "mortally wounded our commander, wounded the [Mississippi River] pilot [M. Douglass], carried away our wheel ropes and cut the signal halyards and took our flag overboard."[197] Huger suffered a severe wound to his groin and immediately summoned Lieutenant Read to assume command. Warley later commented that, after her fight with the *Iroquois*, the *McRae* "was very badly used up."[198]

Following the battle, Commander John DeCamp, commanding officer of the *Iroquois*, would report that "after the fight with *McRae*, *Iroquois* steamed upriver with eight men killed and twenty-four wounded;" her hull had been severely damaged, and "all our boats are smashed, and most of them are not worth repairs."[199] Edward Bacon, the clerk to Commander DeCamp, described the condition of the *Iroquois*, writing home in a letter, that "Her cutwater and bowsprit were carried away; just forward of the smoke stack a shell had struck and carried away her bulwark" and "her appearance was unseaworthy and wretched in the extreme."[200] Both ships had suffered severe damage in the fight.

Lieutenant Huger was taken below to his cabin, and Surgeon Arthur M. Lynch attended to him. In a sense of irony, it was the *USS Iroquois* that Huger was assigned to when he first learned of South Carolina's secession. Huger had tendered his resignation from the United States Navy from her decks while on her initial cruise in the Mediterranean Sea. Lieutenant Read was quickly on the quarterdeck issuing orders to keep the

[196] ORN, ser. 1, vol 18, 332.
[197] Read, 343.
[198] Warley, 90.
[199] ORN, ser. 1, vol 18, 222.
[200] "Letter from Edward W. Bacon to Father", 30 April 1862, Bacon, Edward Woolsey Papers, 1861-1865, manuscript Collections, American Antiquarian Society.

McRae in the fight. After ordering new tiller ropes to be fabricated, Read went below to see Lieutenant Huger for a moment. Huger looked at Read and demanded "Mr. Read, don't surrender my little ship. I have always promised myself that I would fight her until she was under the water!"[201] Read vowed to continue the fight for as long as physically possible.

Returning to the quarterdeck, Read ordered the *McRae* to steer upriver chasing the Union ships that had already passed. The *McRae* rounded the first bend in the river above the forts and discovered eleven Union ships there. Read later wrote that "not deeming it prudent to engage a force so vastly superior to my own, I determined to retire under the guns of the forts."[202] While beginning to turn the ship about, however, Read did engage one Union ship. It was recorded in the deck log of the *USS Kineo*, one of the US Navy ninety-day gunboats under the command of Lieutenant George M. Ransom that mounted four guns, that "the rebel steamer *McRae* came out from behind the point and exchanged shots with us."[203] As the ship turned around to steam downriver, the tiller ropes were again blown away by Union shots, likely from the *Kineo's* guns. The *Kineo* logged that the *McRae* "struck us three times, and we being within range of the fort, turned upstream."[204] Lieutenant Read would not forget the *Kineo*. While withdrawing, the *McRae* slammed into the bank of the river and was unable to back off because of the loss of steering power.

Sailors were immediately dispatched to fix the once again broken tiller ropes while the gunners continued firing at the Union ships steaming upriver. While attempting to fix the *McRae*, Read spotted another Confederate ship slightly upriver from his current position. This proved to be the *Resolute*, part of Captain John Stevenson's River Defense Fleet. The *Resolute* was abandoned and flying a white flag, however, she looked intact and capable of fighting despite also being stuck on the riverbank. Read immediately dispatched Lieutenant Thomas Arnold, who had been wounded earlier in the morning but had stuck with his gun crews, in a small boat "with ten men on board of her with orders to haul down the white flag and fight her guns as long as possible."[205] With Lieutenant

---

[201] Morgan, 73.
[202] ORN, ser. 1, vol 18, 332 – 333.
[203] Ibid., 792.
[204] Ibid., 793.
[205] Ibid., 333.

Arnold went Third Assistant Engineer John Dent to see if he could get the *Resolute's* engine operational and to attempt to get her off the riverbank.

At 07:30 a.m., the *McRae's* guns ceased firing; the single serviceable gun onboard the *Resolute* ceased fire at about the same time. The passing of the forts had been completed and the fighting on April 24 had ended at the forts. A news correspondent onboard the *USS Hartford* noted that "after being under a terrific fire for one hour and twenty minutes we were past the forts."[206] Commander Mitchell sent a tug to help the *McRae* break free of the riverbank. Before it arrived, Read noticed the *Manassas* drifting downriver, abandoned by her crew. A boat was dispatched to the *Manassas* by Read which "ascertained that she was uninjured, but had her injection pipes cut, and that it would be impossible to save her."[207]

At 8:30 am, the *McRae* anchored alongside the incomplete ironclad *Louisiana* and Read began to take reports on the damage done to the ship. Two men onboard, Fireman Michael Fox and Seaman Henry Seymour were killed during the battle. Another seventeen men lay wounded, several mortally. The officers and petty officers suffered considerably compared to the enlisted men. Included among the wounded were Lieutenant Thomas Huger, Lieutenant Thomas Arnold, Pilot M. Douglass, Sailmaker Samuel Hanna, Wardroom Steward James Carr, Fireman First Class George Kendricks, Surgeon's Steward Owen McGrath, and Gunner David Wiltz. These were all good men whose leadership had kept the ship in working order. The wounded enlisted men were Second Class Fireman James Coffey, Watchman Richard Deeble, Seaman John Ryan, Seaman William Ryan, Seaman James Welch, Landsman Francis Hamilton, Landsman John Hays, Coal Heaver Laurens O'Bryan, and Private Charles Rivas.

Damage to the ship itself was heavy. Three shells had penetrated the hull at, or near, the water line. Third Assistant Engineer James Tomb wrote that shells had gone "in on one side and out on the other, leaving holes above the water line large enough to crawl through."[208] Such was the case in the engine room. The steam-driven pumps were now constantly at work pumping water out of the ship. Many grape and canister shot were also jammed into the hull. Reports indicated that "every stay was carried away and three-fourths of the shrouds."[209] A newspaper reporter wrote

---

[206] "The Fleet Runs the Forts," *Harper's Weekly*, May 24, 1862.
[207] Read, 343.
[208] Tomb, 38.
[209] ORN, ser. 1, vol 18, 333.

that "the *McRae* seemed to be everywhere, and that she remained afloat until after the battle was a marvel."[210] One shell and several grape-shot had also penetrated the smokestack causing a severe loss of steam pressure, so the engines were greatly reduced in power. Brigadier General Johnson Duncan, commander of both Forts Jackson and Saint Philip, commented in his report on the battle that "the heroic and gallant manner in which Captain Huger handled and fought the *MacRae* [Sic.] we can all bear evidence.[211] Midshipman Morgan's description was more cynical noting that "her sides were riddled and the heavy projectiles knocked her guns off the carriages and rolled them along the deck crunching the dead and wounded. Her deck was a perfect shambles."[212]

[210] "The Naval Combat in the River," *New Orleans Daily Crescent*, April 29, 1862.
[211] OR, ser. 1, vol. 6, 528.
[212] Morgan, 73.

CHAPTER SEVEN

End on the River

B Y MIDMORNING OF APRIL 24, 1862, Flag Officer Farragut had anchored his flagship, *USS Hartford*, and the rest of the Union ships at Quarantine Station several miles upriver of the forts. His gamble had worked. Of the sixteen ships that Farragut ordered to pass the forts, only one, the *USS Varuna*, had been sunk. Another three ships, the *USS Kennebec*, the *USS Itasca*, and the *USS Winona*, were turned back and did not succeed in passing the forts. However, twelve Union ships had succeeded and were preparing to move on to New Orleans itself. On the Confederate side, things were much worse. Most of the Confederate ships lay on the bottom of the river. Only the warships *Louisiana*, *McRae*, *Jackson*, *Defiance*, and the grounded *Resolute* were still afloat. Added to this were two unarmed tugs, the *W. Burton* and the *Landis*, and one of the two steam launches that were functioning as scouting ships. Casualties in Farragut's squadron numbered two-hundred-ten out of the over four-thousand sailors in his squadron. In Fort Jackson and Fort Saint Philip, there were forty-eight casualties while Confederate naval forces suffered an additional one-hundred-forty-nine casualties on the water.

Lieutenant "Savez" Read ordered damage control parties to make repairs to the *McRae*. He also signaled to Lieutenant Arnold to remain onboard the *Resolute* for the moment and make preparations for getting her off of the riverbank and in full fighting shape. At 10:45, Read sent a quick verbal report to Commander Mitchell onboard the *CSS Louisiana* that the *McRae* was "ready for action, but in very bad condition."[213] It was the only report Mitchell would ever receive about the *McRae's* condition following

---

[213] ORN, ser. 1, vol 18, 346.

the battle. Repairs continued through the day on both sides. Sometime later in the day, the steam launch was dispatched from the *McRae* to scavenge for supplies from two ships of the River Defense Fleet that were sinking along the riverbank upriver from the forts. Third Assistant Engineer John Dent was the engineer onboard the small launch. Another engineer later wrote that "there was a great lot of stores aboard for eating and drinking. Dent brought a lot of it for our mess."[214]

While making repairs to the *McRae*, Lieutenant Read began pondering on what to do with the *Resolute*, which was "was very little injured."[215] He sent a note to Commander Mitchell requesting permission to take the *Resolute* downriver and into the Gulf of Mexico. Read's goal was to unexpectedly run past Porter's ships below the forts and, once in the Gulf of Mexico, commence a raid against Union merchant ships. Unfortunately for Read, the *Resolute* was "attacked by one of the gunboats from above, which succeeded in putting several shots through her hull at the water line."[216] Lieutenant Arnold onboard the *Resolute* estimated that it would take days to get the *Resolute* ready to move, and that would only be if the Union ships halted their attacks upon her. Mitchell then ordered Read to abandon his idea about breaking past the Union ships. He had another assignment for Read and the *McRae*.

Mitchell ordered Read to take most of the officers and crew, except enough to barely keep a functioning watch, and place them onboard the *CSS Louisiana*. Once that was done, the *McRae* would steam upriver past the Union ships, flying a flag of truce, and offload the Confederate sailors that had been wounded in the battle. The trip had been arranged by Lieutenant Warley who received permission for the *McRae* to move from Commander Porter downriver. Commander Mitchell also sent word to Brigadier General Johnson Duncan, in command of the forts, and offered to on load and transport the army's wounded as well. General Duncan accepted and the wounded from the forts, accompanied by Doctor Foster, a civilian doctor who volunteered to help out at Fort Jackson, arrived onboard the *McRae* late in the day on April 25.

The *McRae* departed on the morning of April 26, flying the Confederate flag as well as a white flag at her gaff. Her decks were filled with about forty wounded sailors and soldiers. General Duncan observed that "a

---

[214] Tomb, 40-41.
[215] Wilkinson, 27.
[216] Ibid.

gunboat, with a white flag, dropped down from the Quarantine" to meet the *McRae*.[217] This proved to be the *USS Wissahickson*, another ninety-day gunboat. Her captain, Lieutenant Albert Smith, sent a boat to the *McRae* "ordering her to await the arrival of the *Mississippi*" which was then returning from an upriver reconnaissance.[218] Read then got in a small boat and made his way to the *USS Mississippi*, a paddle wheel frigate. Her executive officer Lieutenant George Dewey, future admiral of the navy and hero in the Spanish-American War, commented in his memoirs that Read came onboard "to get permission to take his dying captain and the other wounded of the *McRae* [and the squadron and forts] to New Orleans."[219] After procuring permission, the *McRae* continued upriver at a snail's pace. Due to the damage to the *McRae's* smokestack in the battle, she could barely defeat the downriver current and continued on rather slowly. Read commented that, on several occasions, he "was frequently obliged to make fast to the bank" until the *McRae* could build up steam to continue the journey upriver.[220] This would not be the last time that her diminished power would be noticed. As the *McRae* moved upriver, she passed many burning wrecks of ships from New Orleans. They had been destroyed to prevent Union forces from capturing them.

Before the *McRae* departed, several officers were offloaded to the *CSS Louisiana*. Lieutenant Thomas Arnold, refusing to move upriver despite his wound, helped take command of the *Louisiana's* gun crews. Lieutenant Thomas Fister joined him in manning the guns. Second Assistant Engineer Henry Fagan and Third Assistant Engineers James Riley, John Dent, and James Tomb reported onboard the *Louisiana* to help install and operate her engines. Joining the officers was the detachment of marines under Sergeant John Seymour ready to man the *Louisiana's* heavy cannon. On April 29, Fagan, Dent, and Tomb were part of an expedition to attempt to move the *Louisiana* into a better position to fire upon the Union ships still below the forts. They would man the tug *Landis* while it towed the *Louisiana* downriver. However, before the maneuver could be executed, "a white flag was raised on the flag staff of the fort [Jackson], and we heard

---

217 OR, Ser. 1, Vol 6, 530.

218 ORN, Ser. 1, Vol 18, 796.

219 George Dewey, *Autobiography of George Dewey: Admiral of the Navy* (New York: Charles Scribner's Sons, 1913), 75.

220 ORN, Ser. 1, Vol 18, 334.

that the forts had surrendered."[221] Union marines would occupy the forts while army forces began the trek upriver to the New Orleans. The plans to tow the *Louisiana* downriver were cancelled and Commander John Mitchell prepared to scuttle her so she could not fall into Union hands.

The *McRae* arrived off of the city of New Orleans at 11:20 on the morning of April 27. Newspapers printed that she "came up to the city from the forts, under a flag of truce, for the purpose of bringing the men wounded during the late bombardment."[222] She let go her anchor between Girod and Julia streets in the American district of the city. For the final miles of her journey upriver, the *USS Cayuga* escorted the *McRae*. This was to ensure that Read reported to Flag Officer Farragut with his intentions. After anchoring, Read immediately reported onboard the *USS Hartford*, Farragut's flagship, and received permission to offload the wounded and to then immediately return to the forts. Once Mayor Monroe learned that the *McRae* was full of wounded, he "sent a request to one of the ferryboats to run along side and convey them to the shore."[223] However, by the time the ship received permission to offload its men, two more of the *McRae's* crew had died. Fireman First Class George Kendricks, who wanted to eat the pig he brought onboard in Missouri, had succumbed to the shell fragment wound of his head, and Gunner David Wiltz also died of his wounds.

By 4:00 pm, all of the wounded had been taken off the ship with the help of the provided ferryboat. Most were sent to the Marine Hospital where local doctors and volunteer nurses tended to them. Read accompanied Lieutenant Huger to his residence, where he was reunited with his fiancée and where doctors attended to him. Read returned to the *McRae* to make preparations to return downriver the next morning. However, at 8:30 pm, the ship began to drag her anchor. Read immediately let go the rest of his anchor chain, which was paid out to its entire fifty fathom length. The ship continued to drag in the rivers current. With no other anchor to let go and with all tugs either downriver at the forts or destroyed at the city wharves, Read's only option was to immediately get the *McRae* underway on her own.

Read wrote in his after action report of the event that he "started the engines and sheered over to the point near the second district ferry

---

[221]   Tomb, 41.

[222]   "Arrival of the Confederate Steamer *McRae*," *New Orleans Daily Crescent*, 28 April 1862.

[223]   "Arrival of the Wounded," *The Daily True Delta*, April 29, 1862.

landing, where the water was shoaler."[224] As the *McRae* crossed the river to the western bank's shoal water, "the ship rested on something under the water, and swung entirely around several times."[225] As a result of striking the underwater object, the *McRae* began to leak badly. By 11:20 pm, water had overcome the furnaces that fed the donkey engine. The men were forced to work pumps manually. The city's police force loaned eleven men of its own to assist in manning the pumps. By 6:00 on the morning of April 28, "the water was six feet in the hold and gaining on us, the vessel was settling rapidly, and the water on the outside was only 2 inches below the shot holes in the ship's sides."[226] The ship was riding dangerously low in the water. Lieutenant Read noted that "the leak was not confined to any particular place, but the water appeared to come through all her seams."[227] The *McRae* was sinking. Read ordered the *McRae* to be abandoned and what was left of the crew piled into the boats and the steam launch. Just before abandoning her, Read cut the *McRae's* injection pipes so she would sink quickly. By 7:00 on the morning of April 28, the *McRae* fell below the river. The next morning, the *New Orleans Daily Picayune* would report that "she sank at her anchorage, opposite the dock yard of Mr. Hughes [Hughes and Company Shipyard in Algiers] on the right [west] bank of the river. All onboard were saved."[228] Another New Orleans paper wrote as an epitaph for the ship that "we were unable to learn positively whether any lives were lost or not; but the general impression was that everybody onboard escaped, as they had plenty of time to do so. The *McRae* was a fine little steamer, and has done good service under the command of the heroic Huger."[229]

The activity was noticed by the Union ships. Captain Henry Bell, Farragut's fleet captain and second in command of the entire naval operation, dispatched a detail of sailors from the *USS Sciota* to the *McRae*. They boarded the abandoned ship as she was sinking and took possession of several documents and letters along with the *McRae's* ensign. Captain Bell noted in his diary that the flag "was ordered to be delivered to Captain [Theodorus] Bailey [onboard the *USS Cayuga*], for him to take [to the

---

[224]   ORN, Ser. 1, Vol 18, 334.
[225]   Ibid.
[226]   Ibid.
[227]   Ibid.
[228]   "The Situation," *New Orleans Daily Picayune*, April 29, 1862.
[229]   "Sinking of the Confederate Steamer *McRae*," *New Orleans Daily Crescent*, April 29, 1862.

Navy Department in Washington D.C.] with the flag of Louisiana hauled down from the city hall."[230] In addition, the deck log of the *USS Sciota* noted on April 28 that a detachment of sailors boarded the *McRae* and "found her abandoned and sinking."[231] The log also noted that several documents were taken in possession by the boarding party and brought to Flag Officer Farragut on the *Hartford*.

As the crew sat on the riverbank, Lieutenant Read returned to the *Hartford* to explain what had happened. Farragut was not present at the time, but the commanding officer of the *Hartford*, Commander Richard Wainwright, heard and accepted Read's explanation. Farragut, however, would later make the claim that Read had intentionally scuttled the ship in violation of the agreement the two men reached when the *McRae* arrived off of the city the day before.

On April 29, Read was making preparations for returning his crew back downriver in the smaller boats from the *McRae*. He even went to see Mayor Monroe to collect any correspondence that he might have for the commanders below. However, while he was visiting the mayor, news arrived that the two forts had surrendered to Commander Porter's ships. Within hours, more news arrived noting that Commander Mitchell had ordered the *Jackson*, *Defiance*, *Resolute*, and the *Louisiana* blown up, and the sailors, including those of the *McRae* that Read had put off, had been taken prisoner on the unarmed tugs *Landis* and *W. Burton*. About 400 sailors and marines surrendered to Union forces. Commander Mitchell allowed several officers to make an attempt to escape capture through the Louisiana swamps. Lieutenant John Wilkinson, onboard the *Louisiana*, later wrote that "those who wished to make the attempt to escape through the bayous, received permission to do so."[232] This included several members of the *McRae's* crew. However, only a handful successfully managed to escape. Read returned to what was left of his crew and informed them that they were no longer returning downriver. Instead, it was now time to escape from the city, which was doomed to surrender to the Union forces.

---

230 ORN, ser. 1, vol 18, 697.
231 ORN, ser. 1 vol 16, 757.
232 Wilkinson, 30.

CHAPTER EIGHT

Fate of the Crew

A FTER THE FIRST UNION SHIPS appeared at the city, all of New Orleans was in a panic. The unfinished ironclad *Mississippi* was blown up after attempts to tow her upriver had failed. Major General Mansfield Lovell ordered all army personnel to evacuate the city by train and make their way to Camp Moore, Louisiana. Some unarmed ships at the city wharves were loaded with supplies and ordered to steam upriver while others were destroyed on the docks in confusion. The crewmen of the *McRae* that were downriver onboard the *Louisiana* were now prisoners. They had no idea what had happened to their ship. One Wisconsin newspaper managed to find testimony from a sailor captured at the forts that the *McRae* "communicated with the federal flag ship, but the result is unknown" and "it is rumored that the federals refused to let her return."[233]

Flag Officer Farragut had to decide the fate of the Confederate forces that had surrendered. He decided that the enlisted men would be set free on parole when they arrived in New Orleans, but the officers, including Lieutenants Arnold and Gift as well as Engineers Tomb, Fagan, Dent, and Riley would be sent to prison camps in the North. The captured sailors from the *McRae* had only what they carried with them for, as Tomb noted, "all of our wardrobe went to the bottom with her [the *McRae*], as we had left everything on board."[234] The captured officers would be imprisoned in Fort Warren in the harbor of Boston, Massachusetts.

---

233 "Latest News, Important from New Orleans," *The Wisconsin Daily Patriot*, April 30, 1862.
234 Tomb, 42.

City Hall of New Orleans Surrendering to Union Forces

Read and the remainder of his crew, no longer bound to return to the forts, took it upon themselves to escape the city in some of the last trains to leave. Young Midshipman Morgan still lay in his sickbed as Farragut passed the forts. Upon learning of the approaching Union ships, Morgan "sprung up, and rushed to the wharf."[235] Not finding a vessel to escape with, he "made his escape from the city with great difficulty" by boarding one of the last trains in New Orleans.[236] He met with other naval officers, among them was Francis W. Dawson, Morgan's future brother-in-law. Morgan and his companions made their way to Richmond to report for duty. The soldiers in New Orleans retreated to Camp Moore, Louisiana, near the Mississippi border on the New Orleans, Jackson, and Great Northern Railroad line, to reorganize. Lieutenant Read and what was left of the *McRae's* crew made their way to Jackson, Mississippi and reported to local naval authorities for reassignment. The crew was fortunate for their quick escape. Within hours of leaving the city, Union sailors lowered the Confederate and Louisiana flags from the New Orleans custom house and

235 Sarah Morgan Dawson, *A Confederate Girl's Diary* (Boston: Riverside Press, 1913), 50.

236 Francis W. Dawson, *Reminisces of Confederate Service 1861 – 1865* (Charleston, SC: New and Courior Book Press, 1882), 43.

city hall, bringing the city under formal occupation. The *McRae* ended its service with the breaking up of the crew for reassignment in Jackson.

Though the *McRae* was sunk, the war would continue for three more years. Her crew would spread out across the Confederacy and the world in their continued naval service. This was not true for Lieutenant Huger, however. He would die from his wounds at 6:00 am May 10, 1862 never having the opportunity to marry his fiancée. One of his last acts was to send a note to Midshipman Morgan stating that "his little brass cannon was 'game to the last'" in the battle at the forts.[237] It was reported that "he was surrounded in his affliction by friends and the best of medical attendance, and nothing was left undone which could possibly tend to mitigate his sufferings or soften his dying pillow."[238] One newspaper reported that there was "an immense and spontaneous gathering of the people of New Orleans" at his funeral.[239] Another paper wrote on May 13, 1862 that "The funeral of Capt. Huger from Christ Church, on Canal street, at 10 o'clock yesterday morning, was attended by a large concourse of our citizens and his brave compatriots in the recent struggle."[240]

Lieutenant Alexander Warley, who had served as the first executive officer of the *McRae* before being transferred to take command of the ironclad *Manassas*, would continue to serve on ironclads. Warley would render good service on the ironclad *Palmetto State* in the Charleston squadron. He would then take command of the *CSS Chicora*, another ironclad stationed in Charleston, in 1863. Warley would later serve as the commander of the *CSS Albemarle*, the famed Confederate ironclad that was built in a cornfield and stood unopposed in coastal North Carolina for much of 1864.

The *McRae's* second executive officer, Lieutenant Charles Read, would have one of the most active careers of all Confederate naval officers. After evacuating New Orleans, he would serve in command of the stern guns on the ironclad *Arkansas*, taking part in her defense of Vicksburg and he was present at her destruction off of Baton Rouge in August of 1862. Read was onboard the *Arkansas* during her movement from the Yazoo River to Vicksburg, where the ship fought against the combined Union fleets of Farragut and Flag Officer Charles H. Davis. During this battle,

---

[237]   Dawson, Sarah, 66.

[238]   "Another Brave Man Gone," *New Orleans Daily Crescent*, May 13, 1862.

[239]   "Death of Lieut. Thomas B. Huger," *Charleston Mercury*, May 20, 1862.

[240]   "Another Brave Man Gone," *New Orleans Daily Crescent*, May 13, 1862.

Read sighted the *USS Kineo* and ensured that she suffered for inflicting damage on the *McRae* on April 24. In fact, one of Read's fellow officers commented that he "treasured the hope of getting alongside the fellow [*USS Kineo*] some day."[241] Following service on the *Arkansas*, Read would be transferred to the commerce raider *CSS Florida*. While off the coast of Brazil in the summer of 1863, Read took command of the *Clarence*, a prize captured by the *Florida*. He would sail across the New England coast in her and two of her prizes, the *Tacony* and the *Archer*. Onboard the *Archer*, he sailed into the harbor of Portland, Maine and cut out the US Revenue Cutter *Caleb Cushing*. Soon after, he was captured and imprisoned in Fort Warren in Boston harbor for over a year. Read took part in the capture of twenty-five Union merchant ships. While imprisoned, he would attempt escape at least three times. Promoted to first lieutenant and receiving the Confederate Medal of Honor for his actions in Maine, Read was exchanged in October of 1864. He served on land batteries in Virginia before leading several commando raids behind Union lines in eastern Virginia. He then commanded the James River squadron's torpedo boats before taking command of the *CSS W.H. Webb* off of Shreveport, Louisiana in March 1865. Read's Civil War career ended when he was forced to beach and burn the *W.H. Webb* in April 1865 while within sight of Fort Jackson after a failed attempt to sneak the ship down the Red and Mississippi Rivers and into the Gulf of Mexico.

Midshipman John Comstock, who left the *McRae* after the Battle of the Head of the Passes, would be promoted to first lieutenant in 1864. Comstock was killed in action while serving on the *CSS Selma* during the Battle of Mobile Bay in August of 1864. Midshipman Henry Marmaduke, who was transferred to the ironclad *Virginia*, also was made a first lieutenant in 1864. He was wounded in the Battle of Hampton Roads in 1862. After recovering from his wound, he served abroad through 1864. Marmaduke returned to the Confederacy and took part in the Battle of Sailor's Creek as a member of the naval infantry brigade that evacuated Richmond with General Robert E. Lee's Army of Northern Virginia.

Lieutenant Thomas Arnold was one of the officers who attempted to escape from the Union forces after the *Louisiana* had been blown up. He was quickly recaptured and would go to Fort Warren in Boston. Exchanged in September 1862, Arnold would then serve onboard the

---

[241] George W. Gift, "The Story of the Arkansas," *Southern Historical Society Papers*, (Richmond, VA, 1887), Vol. 12, 116.

ironclad *Atlanta* and later in the Savannah naval squadron. He resigned from the Confederate Navy on May 16, 1863. Lieutenant Thomas Fister, the volunteer officer on loan from the Revenue Service, was another officer who wished to make an escape through the swamps. Fister was more successful in eluding Union forces, successfully making it to Confederate lines. After discovering that the *Pickens*, his old revenue cutter, was destroyed at the wharves of New Orleans on Farragut's approach, he travelled to Mobile where he served onboard the *CSS Selma*. He would later continue his service in Richmond commanding the naval infantry brigade. Joining Lieutenant Fister in his successful escape through the swamps was Third Assistant Engineer James Riley who would who was sent to the Jackson, Mississippi naval station.

Midshipman James Morgan would also have an eventful career. He would serve onboard the *CSS Chicora*. Sent to England, he then served onboard the commerce raider *Georgia*. Sent back to the Confederacy after the *Georgia's* first cruise, he would graduate from the Confederate Naval Academy and serve among the land installations defending Richmond. He ended the war escorting the family of Confederate President Jefferson Davis out of the capital as it was being evacuated. Morgan would marry the daughter of the former Confederate Secretary of the Treasury and move to Egypt serving as a lieutenant colonel in the Egyptian Army. Midshipman Samuel Blanc would be promoted to master in 1864. Throughout the rest of the war he served onboard the *CSS Baltic, CSS Savannah, CSS Chattahoochee, CSS Nashville, CSS Samson, CSS Hornet,* and *CSS W.H. Webb.* Blanc would also join Morgan as one of the few graduates of the Confederate Naval Academy.

Surgeon Arthur Lynch would serve as the surgeon onboard the *CSS Palmetto State* from the fall of New Orleans to 1864. Lynch was then promoted to be the chief surgeon for the entire Charleston Squadron, and served in that position until the city fell to Union forces. Passed Assistant Surgeon Marcellus Christian would serve at the Richmond Naval Station for the rest of the war, being paroled at Lynchburg, Virginia on May 22, 1865. Second Assistant Engineer Henry Fagan was brought to Fort Warren's prison. After being exchanged, he would serve onboard the *CSS Chattahoochee*, where he was killed on May 30, 1863 when the ship's boilers exploded. Second Assistant Engineer Samuel Brock, who was not liked by his fellow engineers, was reassigned to the Charleston Naval Station. He would resign from the navy within a month of the sinking of the *McRae*.

Third Assistant Engineer John Dent would, after being exchanged from Fort Warren, be promoted to first assistant engineer. He would serve onboard the *CSS Chattahoochee*, the ironclad *Charleston*, and the blockade runner *Coquette*. Dent died of fever on July 15, 1864. Third Assistant Engineer James Tomb would be exchanged in September 1862. He would serve in the torpedo bureau of the Confederate Navy, working on the *CSS David*, assisting in the operations of the submarine *H.L. Hunley*, and laying underwater mines. He would end the war as one of the few sailors promoted to the rank of chief engineer and one of the Confederacy's chief experts on torpedo and mine warfare. Third Assistant Engineer James Riley joined Lieutenant Arnold and managed to escape from the *CSS Louisiana* before it surrendered. He made it to Fort Jackson and joined in the army's surrender, avoiding imprisonment in the north. Riley would then serve at the Jackson, Mississippi naval station.

Records for what happened to most of the enlisted personnel have been lost. However, records do indicate that Seaman Andrew Farraday was transferred to the *CSS North Carolina* where he served as the ironclad's quartermaster. Farraday was listed as part of the crew taken prisoner in the capture of the *CSS Bombshell* in May 5, 1864. One Louisiana newspaper also reported that Seaman Thomas Allen was among a group of prisoners who were brought from New Orleans "for Vicksburg where they will also be exchanged" along with Union prisoners of war in October of 1862.[242] Seaman Allen was brought up to New Orleans with the *McRae* following the battles in April due to ill health. He was brought to the Marine Hospital in the city where he was subsequently taken prisoner when the city came under Union occupation. Boatswain's Mate Thomas Wilson, an Irish immigrant, was advanced to be a warrant officer, serving as the Boatswain of the *CSS Palmetto State*. He participated in the Charleston Squadron's attack on the Union blockading fleet on January 21, 1863. Wilson resigned from the navy on May 23, 1863.

Wardroom Steward James Carr, the young riverboat man from Brooklyn who was accused of being a spy, was transferred to Jackson, Mississippi to recover from the wound to his arm received during the battle. Once recovered, he was transferred to the *CSS Selma* in Mobile. He remained onboard the *Selma* until February 23, 1863 when he and two other men in a small boat discovered "the *[USS] Clifton*, near Horn Island [Alabama], and

---

[242] "Exchange of Prisoners," *Weekly Gazette and Comet*, October 15, 1862.

gave themselves up.[243] Transferred to the *USS Susquehanna* for questioning, young James Carr was released and allowed to return to his family in New York. One month later, another *McRae* sailor would follow him. Coxswain Angus Livingston deserted from the *CSS Tuscaloosa* in April 1863.

Seaman Bernard Allen left the *McRae* and later served on the *CSS Georgia*. Seaman Charles Baker later served on the *CSS Patrick Henry*. Second Class Fireman James Coffey would leave the *McRae* and serve on the *CSS Florida*. He would also join Lieutenant Read on his 1863 raid onboard the *Clarence, Tacony,* and *Archer*. Second Class Fireman Charles Devlin also joined James Coffey and Lieutenant Read on their New England raid. Devlin was exchanged on 18 October 1864. Landsman Patrick Donahoe later served on the *CSS Morgan* in Mobile. First Class Fireman Frank Wilson made his way to Richmond where he was arrested on November 26, 1863 for charges of assault with a knife and disorderly conduct. Landsman Alexander Steward joined on Lieutenant Read's adventures onboard the *Florida, Clarence, Tacony,* and *Archer*. He remained confined in Fort Warren in Boston harbor after the capture of the *Archer* until January 25, 1865 when he was released for taking the oath of allegiance to the United States. Seaman Charles Taylor would serve as a second class fireman on the *CSS Rappahannock* in 1864. Seaman William E. Wilson later served on the *CSS Arctic*. Joining Wilson on the *Arctic* was Seaman John White.

Landsman John Welsh left the shores of New Orleans and headed upriver. He reported onboard the *CSS General Bragg*, which was another of Captain John Stevenson's River Defense Fleet. The *General Bragg* served in the defense of Memphis after the *McRae* returned downriver to New Orleans. Welsh was onboard and participated in the attack on the ironclad *USS Cincinnati* on 10 May 1862. The *General Bragg* was damaged in the attack and Landsman Welsh was mortally wounded in the assault. He died on May 13, 1862.

The case of Ordinary Seaman James H. Kearny was particularly interesting. After leaving New Orleans, he was assigned to the commerce raider *CSS Florida*. He was left behind in Brazil in June 1863 when the ship left port without him. Ordinary Seaman Kearny took a steamer to New Hampshire where he subsequently enlisted in the Third New Hampshire Regiment as a private. That regiment was stationed in Florida in 1864 and

---

[243] ORN, Ser. 1, vol. 19, 627.

Kearny deserted the Union army in March 1864. He subsequently made it to Confederate lines in Savannah, Georgia and returned to service.

Yeoman Richard Morris left the *McRae's* crew and immediately joined the crew of the privateer *F.S. Bartow*. He was captured on May 2, 1862 in New Orleans when the privateer failed to escape from Union forces. Morris was paroled on the spot, but was captured while trying to sneak through Union lines to Confederate forces. He was sent to Fort Jackson, where he was imprisoned for a year.

Several sailors from the *McRae* took part in the Battle of Mobile Bay on August 5, 1864. First Lieutenant John Comstock was killed in the battle onboard the *CSS Selma*. Steward Francis Hamilton, who was arrested by New Orleans Police in early 1862 joined Comstock onboard the *Selma*. He was captured when the ship surrendered during the battle of Mobile Bay. Fireman Second Class John Brady and Ordinary Seaman James Bryant were also both captured during the battle. They had been serving on the ironclad *CSS Tennessee*, Admiral Franklin Buchannan's flagship. Seaman John Edwards was transferred to the *CSS Morgan* and took part in the battle. The *Morgan* escaped and Edwards served on her until she was scuttled May 1865. Seaman Edwards surrendered to Union forces and was paroled at Nanna Hubba Bluff on the Tombigee River in Alabama on May 10, 1865.

Marine Corps records indicate that each member of the marine detachment assigned to the *McRae* was given their parole except for Private Charles Rivas. Rivas had been wounded in the battle on April 24 and was at the Marine Hospital when his fellow marines were captured. Corporal A.W. James, a Virginian, made his way to Virginia where he served until 1865 when he joined Admiral Raphael Semmes naval brigade. James was paroled in Greensboro, North Carolina on April 26, 1865 at the rank of orderly sergeant. Ship's Corporal John O'Neill was sent to the *CSS Baltic*. He was then transferred from the navy back to the Confederate Marine Corps in October 1863, serving at Drewery's Bluff.

Private Michael Bow, from Milkenny Ireland, served in the Richmond, Virginia area into 1864. He was then transferred to Fort Fisher, part of the defenses of Wilmington, North Carolina. Private Bow was mortally wounded and captured in the Second Battle of Fort Fisher on January 15, 1865. He died two days later. Private Timothy Canovan was another crew member that was from a northern state. The Massachusetts native joined the Confederate Marine Corps the day before Fort Sumter was fired on. He served briefly on the *McRae* before being transferred to Pensacola, Florida. Canovan deserted to Union held Fort Pickens on December 22, 1861. He took the oath of allegiance on 26 January, 1862 and was sent back to Massachusetts. Private Frank Gafany deserted from the Marine Corps and subsequently enlisted in Company C of the Thirteenth Louisiana Infantry Regiment. A presidential proclamation was issued in August 1863 that would absolve him of his desertion charge. Private Gafany followed up on the proclamation and returned to the Marine Corps, serving at Drewery's Bluff

The other marines were then held at the Mobile Marine Barracks until exchanged. After that, most were transferred to serve in the vicinity of the capital, Richmond. They rejoined their fellow marines from Marine Corps Company B and took part in the Battle of Drewery's Bluff in 1864 and were part of the naval brigade that took part in the Battle of Sailor's Creek in April 1865. The entire navy and marine force at Sailor's Creek was captured just three days before General Robert E. Lee surrendered the rest of his army.

The *McRae's* crew, however, were not the only ones that had greatly affected its course in history. Major General Mansfield Lovell, who led the defenses of New Orleans, would escape from the city and serve in northern Mississippi, leading a division at the Battle of Corinth. Lovell then went before a board of inquiry regarding the loss of New Orleans. Though the board found no fault on his part, he never received another field command. Brigadier General Johnson Duncan, the leader of Confederate forces at the two forts, served as General Braxton Bragg's chief of staff for the Army of Tennessee. He died of malarial fever on December 18, 1862 in Tennessee. Lieutenant Colonel Edward Higgins, who had taken part in the expedition to capture Ship Island in July 1861 and who had been in command of Fort Jackson, would lead the Twenty-Second Louisiana Infantry Regiment at the siege of Vicksburg where he was captured. Promoted to brigadier general in October 1863, Higgins then led the army defenses of Mobile, Alabama. Commodore George Hollins, the commander of the Mississippi River squadron that called the *McRae* its flagship, reported to Richmond after being relieved. He served on the board of inquiry investigating the destruction of the *CSS Virginia* never receiving another command again. Commander John Mitchell, who led Confederate naval forces defending New Orleans, was given command of the *CSS Albemarle* in 1864. Promoted to the rank of commodore, Mitchell then led the James River Squadron defending Richmond until the fall of the capital.

Captain David Farragut would be named the first admiral in United States naval history as a reward for capturing New Orleans. He would command the Western Gulf Blockading Squadron into 1864. His most famous moment in the war was at the Battle of Mobile Bay, where he ordered Captain Theodorus Bailey onboard the *USS Hartford* to "Damn the torpedoes!" and to attack Confederate forces. Commander David Porter would also be promoted to admiral. After the fall of New Orleans, he took command of the Union gunboats on the Mississippi River helping General Ulysses Grant encircle and capture Vicksburg, Mississippi in 1863. His ships then took part in the Louisiana Red River Campaign in 1864. Porter found himself in charge of the North Atlantic Blockading Squadron in late 1864 and led naval forces in the capture of Fort Fisher, bottling up Wilmington, North Carolina, the last major Confederate port for blockade runners. Major General Benjamin Butler would remain in command of New Orleans for several months. His tenure in command was so notorious that the Confederacy actually placed a bounty on his capture, stating that if he were captured, Butler should be shot on sight. Butler would command a botched effort to capture Richmond and Petersburg, Virginia in 1864 and a failed attempt to capture Wilmington, North Carolina in late 1864. After that, he was removed from command. After the war, Butler would serve as governor of Massachusetts.

The hulk of the *McRae* is still lying in one of the deepest parts of the Mississippi River just off of the city of New Orleans. Her flag was taken north as a trophy of war presented to the United States Department of the Navy. The *McRae's* commissioning pennant, the streamer of cloth that showed that she was in commission for the Confederate Navy, still exists. It is currently on display at the Louisiana Civil War Museum at the Confederate Memorial Hall in New Orleans. This pennant is only one of two commissioning pendants for the Confederate Navy that still exist today, and it is the only surviving pendant using the specifications for commissioning pendants used between 1861 and 1863. A piece of the hull was brought to Sarah Morgan, Midshipman James Morgan's sister. She kept it through the war beside a daguerreotype of Lieutenant Huger.

With the fall of New Orleans, the Confederacy was in dire straits. It had lost its largest city and access to the mouth of the Mississippi River. Edward Pollard, an editor of the Richmond Examiner, wrote in 1866 that "by the capture of New Orleans, he [Admiral Farragut] had secured the great Southern depot of the trade of the immense central valley of the continent."[244] In Richmond, Commodore George Hollins reported to President Davis who told him about the fall of the city. Hollins reportedly barked to the president that he could have prevented the fall of the city if he were allowed to remain in command of the naval forces at New Orleans. It was said that Davis then buried his face in his hands. On April 27, 1862, the French man-of-war *Milan* passed the Union fleet and Forts Jackson and Saint Philip under a flag of truce. Word of the fall of New Orleans then traveled across the Atlantic Ocean. When word reached London, Charles F. Adams, the Union minister to Great Britain, was said to have danced with his son around his office. Word reached France around the same time. The loss of the city made the European powers much more cautious regarding possible recognition of the Confederacy. One southern journalist wrote that "the French government declared that 'if New Orleans had not fallen, our recognition could not have been much longer delayed.'"[245] On May 17, word reached the *USS Constellation* in Spezia, Italy of the fall of New Orleans. Yeoman Moses Safford wrote in his diary that "if this be true the Confederate cause is hopeless."[246] Words such as these spread across the United States and the world.

Combined with assaults from upriver, it now became only a matter of time before the entire Mississippi River fell to Union forces. Most historians of the Civil War believe that once the Confederacy was split in two, it was doomed, and that the loss of New Orleans helped to cause the inevitable collapse of the South. The *CSS McRae* helped to defend New Orleans and the rest of the Mississippi River for the first year of the Civil War. Its actions were commendable and its officers and crew fought hard in battle. Even Union commanders noted that "never did they see so gallant a little ship, or one that fought so desperately as the *McRae*. Men and officers fought like devils."[247]

Perhaps the biggest contribution the *McRae* made to the Confederacy was providing a platform for many officers and crew members to learn their trade and gain experience. After the *McRae* sank, its officers were reassigned across the Confederacy. Men would serve on ironclads, torpedo

---

[244] Edward A. Pollard, *The Southern History of the War: Volume 1* (New York: C.B. Richardson, 1866), 368.

[245] Ibid.

[246] Moses Safford, *The Civil War Naval Diary of Moses Safford, USS Constellation* (Charleston, SC: History Press, 2004), 40.

[247] Dawson, Sarah, 66.

boats, commerce raiders, land installations and blockade runners. They would fight on the Mississippi River, the Gulf of Mexico, the Atlantic coast, and around the world from England to Maine to South America. Its crew would be involved in the most famous battles that the Confederate Navy took part in such as the Battles of Hampton Roads, Drewery's Bluff, Plymouth, Mobile Bay, and Sailor's Creek. The *McRae's* service was distinguished, but not particularly spectacular. Her crew, however, would continue to contribute to the Confederate cause harder than any other organization of men. Men such as Alexander Warley, Charles Read, Thomas Fister, James Morgan, John Dent, and James Tomb contributed everything to the Confederacy and asked for nothing in return. Their service to the Confederate cause was the *McRae's* greatest contribution to the war.

The last mention in official correspondence of the *McRae* was in a letter from Stephen Mallory to Jefferson Davis, dated August 18, 1862. This letter gave details on the condition of the Confederate Navy. In it, Mallory wrote "The conduct of the officers and crew of the *McRae* in these respects has rarely been surpassed in the annals of naval warfare."[248] Mallory went further adding that "Exposed to the terrific fire of many heavy ships, all greatly superior to her in force torn to pieces by their broadsides, her commanding officer, Huger, mortally wounded, and a large portion of her crew killed or wounded, they refused to surrender as long as they could keep her afloat, and she went down without having passed into the enemy's hands."[249]

---

[248] ORN, ser. 2 vol 2, 241.
[249] Ibid.

Muster Roll and Records of the Crew of the *CSS McRae*

Commissioned Officers

Arnold, Thomas
> Born in Arkansas
> Appointed from Arkansas
> Resigned as Midshipman, US Navy, 21 September 1855.
> Lieutenant for the war,
> 18 March 1862. Resigned 16 May 1863.
> *CSS McRae*. Battle of Forts Jackson and Saint Philip (slightly wounded), 24 April 1862. Transferred to *CSS Louisiana* 25 April 1862 (captured). Exchanged 21 September 1862. Jackson Station 1862. *CSS Atlanta*, 1862. *CSS Stono*, 1862-1863.

Comstock, John Henry
> Born in Louisiana
> Appointed from Arkansas
> Resigned as Acting Midshipman, US Navy, 30 January 1861.
> Second Lieutenant, CS Army. First Lieutenant, CS Army, 28 April 1861. Midshipman, 4 May 1861. Lieutenant for the war 8 Feb 1862. Lieutenant, 2 October 1862. First Lieutenant, Provisional Navy, 6 January 1864.
> *CSS McRae*. Commanding *CSS Saint Philip*, 1861-1862. Jackson Station, 1862. Drewery's Bluff, 1862. *CSS Selma*, 1862. *CSS*

> *Morgan* and *CSS Gaines*, 1862-1863. Special Service, 1863-1864.
> *CSS Selma*, 1864. Battle of Mobile Bay (killed), 5 August 1864.

Douglass, M.

> River Pilot
> *CSS McRae*; defense of Fort Jackson and Saint Philip
> (Severely Wounded), 24 April 1862.

Dunnington, John W.

> Born in Kentucky
> Appointed from Kentucky
> Resigned as Lieutenant, US Navy, 25 April 1861. First
> Lieutenant, 2 May 1861. Colonel, CS Army, 1862.
> *CSS McRae*. Commanding *CSS Tuscarora* when destroyed
> 23 November 1861. *CSS Calhoun*, 1861. *CSS Mason*, 1862;
> Commanding *CSS Pontchartrain*, 1862-1863. Participated in
> defense and surrender of Arkansas Post (captured), 12 January
> 1863. Exchanged 5 May 1863. Commanding blockade runner
> *Owl*, 1864. Commanding *CSS Virginia II*, 1864-1865. Semmes
> Naval Brigade, 1865. Paroled at Greensboro, North Carolina, 26
> April 1865.

Eggleston, John R.

> Born in Virginia
> Appointed from Mississippi
> Resigned as Lieutenant, US Navy, 22 January 1861. First
> Lieutenant, 5 April 1861.
> *CSS McRae*. *CSS Virginia*, 1862. Battle of Hampton Roads,
> 8-9 March 1862. Drewery's Bluff, 1862. Flag Lieutenant,
> Mobile Squadron, 1862-1864. Mobile Station, 1864-1865.
> Paroled at Jackson, Mississippi, 14 May 1865.

Foster

> Civilian Doctor
> Transferred to *CSS McRae*, 26 April 1862.

Fister, Thomas D.

> Born in Pennsylvania
> Lieutenant, CS Revenue Service.
> *CSRC Pickens* and *CSRC Morgan*, 1861. *CSS McRae*, 1862.
> Battle of Forts Jackson and Saint Philip, 24 April 1864.
> Transferred to *CSS Louisiana*, 25 April 1862. Escaped capture

through Louisiana swamps. Richmond Station, 1862-1863.
Mobile Station, 1863-1865.

Freeman, Virginius
Born in Virginia
Appointed from Virginia
Former First Assistant Engineer, US Navy. Chief Engineer,
16 July 1861.
CSS McRae. New Orleans Station, 1861-1862. Jackson Station,
1862. *CSS Stono,* 1863. Charlotte, North Carolina, 1865.
Paroled at Greensboro, North Carolina, 28 April 1865.

Gift, George W.
Born in Tennessee
Appointed from Tennessee
Resigned as Midshipman, US Navy, 10 January 1851. Acting
Master, 27 December 1861. Appointed Lieutenant for the war 18
March 1862. First Lieutenant, Provisional Navy, 6 January 1864.
CSS New Orleans, 1861. *CSS McRae,* Battle of Forts Jackson and
Saint Philip, 24 April 1862. Transferred to *CSS Louisiana,* 25
April 1862. *CSS Arkansas,* 1862. *CSS Chattahoochee,* 1862-1863.
CSS Baltic and *CSS Gaines,* Mobile Station, 1863. Johnsons
Island Expedition, 1863. Commanding *Ranger,* 1864. *USS
Underwriter* capture, 2 February 1864. Commanding *CSS
Chattahoochee,* 1864. *CSS Savannah,* 1864. *CSS Tallahassee,*
1864. Paroled at Albany, Georgia, 22 May 1865.

Henderson, Richard H.
Born in Washington, D.C.
Appointed from Virginia
First Lieutenant, CS Marine Corps, 16 April 1861.
CSS McRae. Pensacola, 1861. Richmond Station, 1861-1862.
CSS Patrick Henry, 1862 and1863. Battle of Hampton Roads,
8-9 March 1862. Charleston Station, 1862-1863. Drewery's
Bluff, 1863 and 1864. *CSS Raleigh* and *CSS Arctic,* Wilmington
Station, 1864. Richmond Station, 1864-1865.

Huger, Thomas Bee
Born in South Carolina
Appointed from South Carolina
Resigned as Lieutenant, US Navy, 11 January 1861. First
Lieutenant, 28 March 1861.

Commanding Battery on Morris Island, 1861. Battle of Fort Sumter, 12-13 April 1861. Commanding *CSS McRae*, 1861-1862. Battle of Head of the Passes, 12 October 1861. Defense of New Madrid, Missouri, 3-13 March 1862. Battle of Forts Jackson and Saint Philip (mortally wounded in groin and shoulder), 24 April 1862. Died 10 May 1862.

Lynch, Arthur M.

Born in South Carolina

Appointed from South Carolina

Resigned as Passed Assistant Surgeon, US Navy, 14 January 1861. Surgeon, 26 March 1861.

Charleston Station, 1861. *CSS McRae*, 1861-1862. Savannah Station, 1862. *CSS Palmetto State*, Charleston Station, 1863-1864. Blockading Squadron Attack, 31 January 1863. *CSS Savannah*, Savannah Station, 1864. Fleet Surgeon, Charleston Station, 1864.

Read, Charles W.

Born in Mississippi

Appointed from Mississippi

Resigned as Midshipman, US Navy, 4 February 1861. Acting Midshipman, 13 April 1861. Acting Master, 12 July 1861. Lieutenant, 8 February 1862. First Lieutenant, Provisional Navy, 6 January 1864.

CSS McRae, 1861-1862. Battle of Head of Passes, 12 October 1861. Defense of New Madrid, Missouri, 3-13 March 1862. Battle of Forts Jackson and Saint Phillip, 24 April 1862. Commanding *CSS McRae* following wounding of Lieutenant Huger 24 April 1862. *CSS Arkansas*, 1862. Passage from Yazoo River to Vicksburg, 15 July 1862. *CSS Florida*, 1862. Commanding *CSS Clarence*, *CSS Tacony*, *CSS Archer* Expedition, 1863 (captured 27 June 1863). Exchanged 18 October 1864. Commanding torpedo boats, James River Squadron, 1865. Commanding *CSS W.H. Webb.* (captured 24 April 1865). Released and paroled 24 July 1865.

Sample

Paymaster

CSS McRae

Warley, Alexander F.
> Born in South Carolina
> Appointed from South Carolina
> Resigned as Lieutenant, US Navy, 24 December 1860. First Lieutenant, 26 March 1861.
> Morris Island Batteries, Charleston, South Carolina, 1861. *CSS McRae*, 1861. Commanding *CSS Manassas*, 1861-1862. Battle of Head of Passes, 12 October 1861. Battle of Forts Jackson and Saint Philip, 24 April 1862 (captured). Exchanged 5 August 1862. *CSS Palmetto State*, Charleston Station 1862. *Commanding CSS Chicora*, Charleston Station, 1862-1863. *CSS Harriet Lane*, 1863. Commanding *CSS Water Witch*, 1864. Commanding *CSS Albemarle* when destroyed, 28 October 1864. Wilmington Station, 1864. Captured and paroled at Athens, Georgia, 8 May 1865.

Warrant Officers

Albright, E.
> Born in Louisiana
> Appointed from Louisiana
> Paymaster's Clerk, 29 June 1861.
> *CSS McRae*, 1861. *CSS Virginia*, 1862. Richmond Station, 1862-1864.

Blanc, Samuel Peters
> Born in Louisiana
> Appointed from Louisiana
> Acting Midshipman, 29 August 1861. Passed Midshipman, 8 January 1864. Master in Line of Promotion, Provisional Navy, 2 June 1864.
> *CSS McRae*, 1861-1862. Battle of Forts Jackson and Saint Philip, 24 April 1862. Jackson Station, 1862. Fort Polk, 1862. *CSS Baltic*, Mobile Station, 1862-1863. *CSS Savannah*, Savannah Station, 1863. *CSS Patrick Henry*, 1863. *CSS Chattahoochee*, 1864. *CSS Nashville*, 1864. *CSS Sampson*, 1864. Commanding *CSS Hornet*, 1865. *CSS W.H. Webb* (captures 24 April 1865). Released and Paroled 13 June 1865.

Brock, Samuel
> Second Assistant Engineer, 21 September 1861. Resigned 24 May 1862.
> *CSS Carondelet*, 1861. *CSS Tuscarora*, 1861. *CSS McRae*, 1862. Defense of Fort Jackson and Saint Philip, 24 April 1862. Charleston Station, 1862.

Choisy, A. McDowell
> Master's Mate, 5 February 1862. Captain's Clerk, 8 April 1862.
> *CSS McRae*, 1862. Jackson Station, 1862.

Christian, Marcellus P.
> Born in Virginia
> Appointed from Virginia
> Formerly Assistant Surgeon, US Navy. Assistant Surgeon, 18 July 1861. Passed Assistant Surgeon, 25 October 1862.
> Culpepper Court House Hospital, 1861. *CSS Huntress*, 1861. *CSS McRae*, 1862. Richmond Station, 1862-1864. Paroled at Lynchburg, 22 May 1865.

Collins, Bernard J.
> First Assistant Engineer.
> *CSS McRae*, 1861. New Orleans Station, 1861-1862. Jackson Station, 1862.

Darcy, John J.
> Appointed from South Carolina
> Second Assistant Engineer, 5 June 1861. First Assistant Engineer, 15 August 1863.
> *CSS McRae*, 1861-1862. Jackson Station, 1862. *CSS Huntress* and *CSS Palmetto State*, Charleston Station, 1862-1864.

Dent, John H.
> Born in Alabama
> Appointed from Alabama
> Acting Third Assistant Engineer, 11 May 1861. Second Assistant Engineer, 21 May 1863.
> *CSS McRae*, 1861-1862. Battle of Forts Jackson and Saint Philip, 24 April 1862. Transferred to *CSS Louisiana*, 25 April 1862 (captured). Exchanged 5 August 1862. *CSS Chattahoochee*, 1862-1863. *CSS Hampton*, 1863. *CSS Charleston*, 1863-1864. *Coquette*, 1864.

Fagan, Henry
>Born in Florida
>Appointed from Washington, D.C.
>Formerly Third Assistant Engineer, US Navy. Entry into
>CS Navy 23 July 1861. Acting Second Assistant Engineer,
>25 November 1861.
>*CSS McRae*, 1861-1862. Battle of Forts Jackson and Saint Philip,
>24 April 1862. Transferred to *CSS Louisiana*, 25 April 1862
>(captured). Paroled 31 July 1862. *CSS Chattahoochee*, 1862-1863
>(killed after boiler explosion onboard on 27 May 1863).

Gottheil, Edward.
>Appointed from Louisiana
>Acting Master, 30 January 1862. Resigned 4 April 1862.
>*CSS McRae*, 1862.

Hanna, Samuel
>Ordinary Seaman. Sailmaker
>*CSS McRae*. Battle of Forts Jackson and Saint Philip, 24 April
>1862 (wounded in head and shoulder).

Hollins, George N. Jr.
>Third Assistant Engineer, 19 September 1861. Acting Second
>Assistant Engineer, 1 November 1861.
>*Saint Nicholas*, 1861. *CSS Florida*, 1861. *CSS New Orleans*, 1861.
>*CSS McRae*, 1861. *CSS Ivy*, 1861-1862. *CSS Richmond*, 1862.
>Died 5 September 1862.

Hutchinson, Samuel W.
>Appointed from Louisiana
>Paymaster's Clerk. Captain's Clerk, 1 May 1862. Assistant
>Paymaster.
>*CSS Sumter*, 1861. *CSS McRae*, 1861-1862. *CSS Mobile*, 1862.
>Jackson Station, 1862-1863.

Jackson, William Hutchenson
>Born in Virginia
>Appointed from Maryland
>Third Assistant Engineer, 5 June 1861. Second Assistant Engineer,
>27 August 1862. Resigned 26 June 1863. Acting Second Assistant
>Engineer, 3 July 1864. Resigned 4 August 1864.
>*CSS McRae* and *CSS Jackson*, 1861-1862. *CSS Arkansas*, 1862.
>Breakthrough from Yazoo River to Vicksburg (wounded in head

and hand), 15 July 1862. *CSS Florida*, 1862-1863. *CSS Chicora*, 1863. Service Abroad, 1863-1864. *CSS Stonewall*, 1865.

Jordan, Charles W.

Born in Virginia

Appointed from Virginia

Formerly Third Assistant Engineer, US Navy, Stricken from rolls 6 May 1861. Third Assistant Engineer, 11 June 1861. Second Assistant Engineer, 27 August 1862. First Assistant Engineer, 15 August 1863.

CSS Jackson and *CSS McRae*, 1861-1862. Jackson Station, 1862. *CSS Beaufort*, 1862. *CSS Selma*, 1862-1863. *CSS Nansemond*, 1863-1864. *CSS Albemarle*, 1864. Wilmington Station, 1864-1865. Semmes' Naval Brigade, 1865. Paroled at Greensboro, North Carolina, 28 April 1865.

Levine, William T.

Appointed from Louisiana

Acting Master, 19 October 1861.

CSS McRae, 1861-1862. *CSS Manassas*, 1862. Battle of Forts Jackson and Saint Philip, 24 April 1862. Jackson Station, 1862.

Levy, Charles H.

Born in Virginia

Appointed from Virginia

Formerly Second Assistant Engineer, US Navy, Dismissed July 1861. Second Assistant Engineer, 2 July 1861. Acting First Assistant Engineer, 25 November 1861. Chief Engineer, Provisional Navy, 26 October 1864.

CSS Jackson and *CSS McRae*, 1861-1862. Admitted to *CSS Saint Philip* hospital ship from 25 November 1861 to 20 December 1861 for intermittent fever. Jackson Station, 1862. Charleston Station, 1862. *CSS Richmond*, 1863. *CSS Stono*, 1863-1864. *CSS Tallahassee*, 1864. *CSS Chickamauga*, 1864.

Loper, John H.

Born in South Carolina

Appointed from South Carolina

First Assistant Engineer, 23 April 1861.

CSS McRae. New Orleans Station, 1861-1862. Jackson Station, 1862. Charleston Station, 1862. *CSS Spray*, 1862-1864. Paroled at Saint Marks, Florida on 12 May 1865.

Marmaduke, Henry Hungerford
> Born in Missouri
> Appointed from Missouri
> Resigned as Acting Midshipman, US Navy, 18 March 1861.
> Midshipman, 8 May 1861. Master in Line of Promotion, 4
> October 1862. Lieutenant, 24 August 1863. First Lieutenant,
> Provisional Navy, 6 January 1864.
> *CSS McRae*, 1861. Battle of Head of Passes, 12 October 1861.
> *CSS Virginia*, 1861-1862. Battle of Hampton Roads (wounded
> in arm), 8-9 March 1862. *CSS Chattahoochee*, 1862-1863.
> Service Abroad, 1863-1864. Commanding *CSS Sampson*, 1864.
> *CSS Columbia* and *CSS Chicora*, 1865. Tucker's Naval Brigade,
> Richmond Station. Battle of Sailor's Creek (wounded and
> captured), 6 April 1865. Released 20 June 1865.

Morgan, James Morris
> Born in Louisiana
> Appointed from Louisiana
> Resigned as Acting Midshipman, US Navy, 16 April 1861.
> Acting Midshipman, 8 June 1861. Midshipman, 8 July 1861.
> *CSS McRae*. Battle of Head of Passes, 12 October 1861. Admitted
> to CSS Saint Philip hospital ship from 6 December 1861 to
> 20 December 1861 for fever. Battle of New Madrid (slightly
> wounded), 3-13 March 1862. Drewery's Bluff, 1862. *CSS Chicora*,
> 1862. Service Abroad, 1862-1863. *CSS Georgia*, 1863-1864.
> *CSS Patrick Henry*, 1864. James River Batteries, 1864-1865.
> Accompanied Mrs. Jefferson Davis out or Richmond, April 1865.

Riley, James H.
> Acting Third Assistant Engineer, 23 September 1861.
> Resigned 8 November 1861. Acting Third assistant Engineer,
> 14 January 1862.
> *CSS Jackson* and *CSS Livingston*, 1861. *CSS McRae*, 1862.
> Transferred to *CSS Louisiana*, 25 April 1862. Escaped capture
> through Louisiana swamps. Jackson Station, 1862.

Stone, Sardine Graham, Jr.
> Born in Alabama
> Appointed from Alabama
> Resigned as Acting Midshipman, US Navy, 16 January
> 1861. Acting Midshipman, 13 April 1861. Acting Master,

24 September 1861. Lieutenant, 28 February 1862. First
Lieutenant, Provisional Navy, 6 January 1864.
CSS Morgan, *CSS McRae*, *CSS Manassas*, and *CSS General
Polk*, 1861-1862. Battle of Head of Passes, 12 October 1861.
Jackson Station, 1862. *CSS Baltic*, 1862. *CSS Florida*, 1862-
1864. Captured on 7 October 1864 in Brazil. Released
25 January 1865.

Thomas, Philip
Appointed from Maryland
Third Assistant Engineer, June 1861.
CSS McRae, 1861. Fell overboard and drowned, 14 July 1861.

Tomb, James H.
Born in Florida
Appointed from Florida
Third Assistant Engineer, 21 June 1861. Second Assistant
Engineer, 5 September 1862. First Assistant Engineer, 15 August
1863. Chief Engineer, 5 October 1863.
CSS Jackson, 1861. *CSS McRae*, 1862. Battle of Forts Jackson
and Saint Philip, 24 April 1862. Transferred to *CSS Louisiana*
25 April 1862 (captured). Exchanged 5 August 1862. *CSS
Chicora* and *CSS Juno*, 1862-1864. Blockading Squadron
Attack, 31 January 1863. Attack on *USS Ironsides*, 5 October
1863. Torpedo Service, Savannah Squadron, 1864-1865. Paroled
at Tallahassee, Florida, 16 May 1865.

Wiltz, David C.
Gunner
CSS McRae. Battle of Forts Jackson and Saint Philip,
24 April 1865 (mortally wounded). Died shortly after battle.

Zimmerman, Frank
Ordinary Seaman. Ship's Steward, 1 April 1862.
CSS McRae.

Petty Officers

Butler, William
Born in New Jersey
Wardroom Cook. Landsman. Steward.

CSS McRae. Sent to *CSS Saint Phillip* hospital ship from 27 December 1861 to 31 January 1862 for fracture. *CSS Morgan*, 1862-1863. *CSS Arctic*, 1863-1864. *CSS Morgan*, 1865.

Carleton, George W.
> Born in Missouri
> Acting Master's Mate, 2 April 1862. Paymaster's Clerk.
> *CSS McRae*, 1862. Jackson Station, 1862. *CSS Chicora* and *CSS Palmetto State*, 1863-1864.

Carlon, Bernard
> Ordinary Seaman. Quarter Gunner.
> *CSS McRae.*

Carr, James
> Born in New York
> Wardroom Steward.
> *CSS Ivy*, 1861. *CSS McRae*. Battle of Forts Jackson and Saint Philip, 24 April 1862 (wounded in left arm). Jackson Station, 1862. *CSS Selma*, 1862-1863. Deserted to the *USS Clifton* on 23 February 1863 and returned to New York.

Clough, Alvaro
> Born in Ireland
> Seaman. Carpenter's Mate.
> *CSS McRae*. Sent to *CSS Saint Philip* hospital ship from 12 January 1862 to 21 January 1862 for dysentery.

Condon, Michael
> First Class Fireman.
> *CSS McRae.*

Dassel, Charles
> Seaman. Quarter Gunner.
> *CSS McRae.*

Henry, Thomas
> Born in Ireland
> First Class Fireman
> *CSS McRae*. Sent to Charity Hospital, New Orleans, on 3 November 1861 for syphilis. Sent to *CSS Saint Philip* hospital ship from 7 December 1861 to 22 December 1861 for fever. Sent to *CSS Saint Philip* hospital ship on 15 April 1862 for syphilis.

Kendricks, George
> Ordinary Seaman. First Class Fireman
> *CSS McRae*. Battle of Forts Jackson and Saint Philip
> (mortally wounded in head).

Livingston, Angus
> Seaman. Captain of Foretop. Coxswain.
> *CSS McRae*. *CSS Tuscaloosa*, 1863. Deserted, April 1863.

McDonald, James
> Born in Scotland
> First Class Fireman
> *CSS McRae*. Sent to Charity Hospital, New Orleans, from
> 3 November 1861 to 30 November 1861 for fever.

McDonald, John
> Captain of Foretop.
> *CSS McRae*. Mobile Station, 1862.

McGadock, John
> Seaman. Captain of Afterguard.
> *CSS McRae*.

McGrath, Owen
> Landsman. Surgeon's Steward.
> *CSS McRae*. Defense of Fort Jackson and Saint Philip
> (slightly wounded), 24 April 1862.

McGrath, Thomas
> Seaman. Boatswain's Mate, 1861.
> *CSS McRae*, 1861-1862. Died 3 April 1862.

McGuire, John
> Landsman. Second Class Fireman. First Class Fireman, 20
> November 1861.
> *CSS McRae*.

Morris, Richard
> Landsman. Yeoman.
> *CSS McRae*. Privateer F.S. Bartow, 1862. Captured and paroled,
> 2 May 1862. Imprisoned at Fort Jackson for one year after
> attempting to move through Union lines to Confederate forces.

Newman, P.G.
> Carpenter's Mate.
> *CSS McRae*.

O'Neill, John
> Private, CSMC, 6 April 1861. Transferred to CS Navy 1
> September 1861. Ship's Corporal. Seaman. Private, CSMC,
> 10 October 1863.
> *CSS McRae*, 1861-1862. Battle of Forts Jackson and Saint Philip,
> 24 April 1862. Transferred to *CSS Louisiana*, 25 April 1862.
> Captured and paroled. *CSS Baltic*, 1863. Drewery's Bluff, 1863

Rankin, John
> Landsman. Wardroom Steward.
> *CSS McRae*.

Robenson, James
> First Class Fireman.
> *CSS McRae*. Deserted February 1862. Returned to *CSS McRae*
> on 2 February 1862.

Rohman, Thomas
> Quartermaster
> *CSS McRae*.

Williams, William
> First Class Fireman.
> *CSS McRae*.

Wilson, Thomas
> Born in Ireland
> Boatswain's Mate. Boatswain. Resigned, 29 May 1863.
> *CSS McRae*. Sent to Charity Hospital from 3 November 1861 to
> 26 November 1861 for fever. *CSS Palmetto State*, 1863. Attack
> on Blockading Fleet, 31 January, 1863.

Wilson, Frank
> First Class Fireman
> *CSS McRae*. Arrested in Richmond, Virginia on 26 November
> 1863 on charges of assault and disorderly conduct.

Enlisted Sailors

Allen, Bernard
> Born in Louisiana
> Ordinary Seaman. Seaman. Gun Captain.
> *CSS McRae*. Sent to Charity Hospital, New Orleans, on 3
> November 1861 for fever. *CSS Georgia*.

Allen, Thomas
> Seaman.
> *CSS McRae.* Sent to Marine Hospital, New Orleans, on 28 April 1862. Captured upon surrender of New Orleans. Exchanged in October 1862.

Andrews, Richard
> Seaman.
> *CSS McRae.* Sent to *CSS Saint Philip* hospital ship on 29 September 1861 for fever. Discharged from navy on 20 December 1861.

Babcock, William
> Ordinary Seaman.
> *CSS McRae.*

Baker, Charles
> Seaman. Landsman.
> *CSS McRae.* Sent to *CSS Saint Philip* hospital ship from 30 October 1861 to 20 December 1861 for fever.
> *CSS Patrick Henry,* 1864.

Barnes, George, Jr.
> Landsman.
> *CSS McRae. CSS Virginia,* 1862.

Barry, James
> First Class Boy.
> *CSS McRae,* 1861. *CSS Jackson,* 1862.

Bates, John
> Seaman.
> *CSS McRae.,* 1861. Deserted on 18 November 1861.

Beber, William
> Ordinary Seaman.
> *CSS McRae. CSS Huntress,* 1862.

Booth, Thomas
> Seaman.
> *CSS McRae.*

Brady, John
> Coal Heaver. Second Class Fireman, 20 November 1861.
> *CSS McRae. CSS Tennessee,* 1864. Battle of Mobile Bay (captured), 5 August 1864.

Brown, John
>
> Seaman.
>
> *CSS McRae. CSS Pontchartrain*, 1862. *CSS Baltic*, 1862-1863.
> *CSS Tuscaloosa*, 1863-1864.

Brown, Thomas
>
> Ordinary Seaman.
>
> *CSS McRae*, 1861. Deserted 19 December 1861.

Bryant, James
>
> Ordinary Seaman.
>
> *CSS McRae. CSS Tennessee*, 1864. Battle of Mobile Bay
> (captured), 5 August 1864.

Bush, Peter
>
> Landsman. Ordinary Seaman.
>
> *CSS McRae.*

Campion, John.
>
> Born in Ireland
>
> Second Class Fireman.
>
> *CSS McRae.* Sent to Charity Hospital on 3 November 1861 for
> fever.

Clayton, George
>
> Ordinary Seaman.
>
> *CSS McRae.*

Coffey, James
>
> Second Class Fireman
>
> *CSS McRae.* Battle of Forts Jackson and Saint Philip
> (wounded), 24 April 1862. *CSS Florida*, 1862. *CSS Clarence*,
> *CSS Tacony, CSS Archer* Expedition, 1863 (captured 27 June
> 1863).

Collins, Peter, E.
>
> Landsman.
>
> *CSS McRae.*

Crawley, Charles
>
> Ordinary Seaman.
>
> *CSS McRae.*

Creighton, John
>
> Landsman.
>
> *CSS McRae.*

Deeble, Richard
Born in Louisiana
Watchman.
CSS McRae. Battle of Forts Jackson and Saint Philip (wounded in calf), 24 April 1862.

Devlin, Charles
Born in Scotland
Landsman. Second Class Fireman.
CSS McRae. Deserted on 18 November 1861. Returned to duty by 26 November 1861. Sent to *CSS Saint Philip* hospital ship from 7 December 1861 to 3 February 1862 for fever. Jackson Station, 1862. *CSS Florida*, 1862. *CSS Clarence, CSS Tacony, CSS Archer* Expedition, 1863 (captured 27 June 1863). Exchanged 18 October 1864.

Dixon, Henry
Seaman.
CSS McRae.

Donahoe, Patrick
Landsman. Coal Heaver. Second Class Fireman,
20 November 1861.
CSS McRae. CSS Huntsville, 1863. *CSS Morgan*, 1863-1864.

Edwards, John
Ordinary Seaman. Seaman.
New Orleans Station, 1861. *CSS McRae. CSS Morgan*, 1865. Paroled at Nanna Hubba Bluff, Tombigee River, Alabama, 10 May 1865.

Ellis, James
Seaman. Boatswain's Mate.
CSS McRae, 1861. New Orleans Station, 1861.

Farraday, Andrew
Born Ireland
Seaman. Quartermaster.
CSS McRae. CSS North Carolina, 1862. *CSS Bombshell*, 1864. Captured onboard *CSS Bombshell* on 5 May 1864.

Fitzmorris, John
Landsman.
CSS McRae.

Flaherty, Andrew
Seaman.
CSS McRae. Sent to *CSS Saint Philip* hospital ship on 20
December 1861 for fever.

Folly, Jackson
Seaman.
CSS McRae.

Fox, Michael
Fireman.
CSS McRae. Battle of Forts Jackson and Saint Philip
(killed, struck by shell), 24 April 1862.

Francisco, Columbus
Landsman.
CSS McRae.

Gibbs, George
Landsman. Coal Heaver. Second Class Fireman,
20 November 1861.
CSS McRae. Arrested by New Orleans Police and returned to
naval authorities on 17 February 1862.

Given, Robert
Born in New York
Landsman.
CSS McRae. Sent to *CSS Saint Philip* hospital ship from 27
December 1861 to 31 January 1862 for catarrhs.

Glynn, John
Landsman.
CSS McRae. Sent to Marine Hospital, New Orleans, 28 April
1862.

Gregory, Nicholas
Seaman.
CSS McRae. Died 6 March 1862.

Grinder, Nels
Landsman.
CSS McRae.

Guster, George A.
Seaman.
CSS McRae.

Hamilton, Francis F.
>Landsman. Seaman. Steward.
>*CSS McRae*. Arrested by New Orleans Police, 30 January 1862, but was returned to *CSS McRae*. Battle of Forts Jackson and Saint Philip (slightly wounded), 24 April 1862. *CSS Selma*, 1862-1864. Battle of Mobile Bay (captured), 5 August 1864.

Hays, John
>Landsman. Seaman.
>*CSS McRae*. Battle of Forts Jackson and Saint Philip (wounded in head), 24 April 1862. *CSS Isondiga*, 1863-1864.

Hoes, Rand
>Third Class Boy
>*CSS McRae*.

Hynes, William
>Landsman.
>*CSS McRae*.

Jones, Ed.
>Born in Maryland
>Landsman. Seaman.
>*CSS McRae*. Sent to *CSS Saint Philip* hospital ship of 20 November 1861 for rheumatism. Discharged from navy on 1 January 1862 for rheumatism.

Kearny, James H.
>Ordinary Seaman. Private, US Army.
>*CSS McRae*. *CSS Florida*, 1862-1863. Left behind in Brazil, June 1863, and made his way to New Hampshire. Enlisted in Third New Hampshire Regiment, US Army. Deserted US Army, March 1864. Reported to Savannah Station, 1864.

Keen, James
>Born in Ireland
>Died 20 June 1861 due to fractured skull that was inflicted when he fell off a yard-arm and struck a wharf.

Kern, Armand
>Ordinary Seaman.
>*CSS McRae*.

Killan, Patrick
>Coal Heaver. Second Class Fireman, 20 November 1861.
>*CSS McRae*.

Kirk, Samuel
>Second Class Fireman
>*CSS McRae.*

Larkin, Thomas
>Landsman.
>*CSS McRae.*

Littig, Charles
>Seaman. Quartermaster.
>*CSS McRae. CSS Pontchartrain*, 1862-1863.

Marmion, John
>Landsman.
>*CSS McRae.*

Maynard, Charles
>Landsman. Steward.
>*CSS McRae.*

McBride, Francis
>Ordinary Seaman
>*CSS McRae.* Sent to *CSS Saint Philip* hospital ship from
>29 October 1861 to 14 November 1861 for fever. Jackson
>Station, 1862.

McBride, Thomas.
>Born in Alabama
>Ordinary Seaman.
>*CSS McRae.* Sent to *CSS Saint Philip* hospital ship from
>10 November 1861 to 20 December 1861 for syphilis. *CSS
>Jackson*, 1862.

McDonald, John T.
>Seaman. Boatswains Mate.
>*CSS McRae. CSS Pontchartrain*, 1862-1863.

McGlone, James
>Seaman. Boatswains Mate
>*CSS McRae.* Jackson Station, 1862. *CSS Huntsville*, 1863.

McKenzie, Andrew
>Ordinary Seaman.
>*CSS McRae.*

McNevin, John
>Landsman.
>*CSS McRae.*

McTee, James
> Seaman.
> *CSS McRae.*

Miller, John
> *CSS McRae*, 1862. Discharged from navy 10 February 1862.

Murtha, Thomas
> Born in England
> Ordinary Seaman
> *CSS McRae.* Sent to Charity Hospital, New Orleans, on 3
> November 1861 for fever.

Myers, James
> Seaman.
> *CSS McRae.* Sent to *CSS Saint Philip* hospital ship,
> 21 December 1861. Died on 25 December 1861 of pleurisy.

Newman, William
> Seaman.
> *CSS McRae*, 1861. Deserted 19 December 1861.

Nolan, Patrick
> Landsman. Coal Heaver. Second Class Fireman,
> 20 November 1861.
> *CSS McRae.* Jackson Station, 1862.

O'Bryan, Laurens
> Coal Heaver.
> *CSS McRae.* Battle of Forts Jackson and Saint Philip
> (slightly wounded), 24 April 1862.

Parker, James
> Born in England
> Seaman.
> *CSS McRae.* Sent to *CSS Saint Philip* hospital ship on
> 29 October 1861 for fever. Discharged from navy on
> 8 February 1862 for intermittent fever.

Quinn, Edward
> Coal Heaver.
> *CSS McRae.* Mobile Station, 1862.

Roach, William
> Ordinary Seaman.
> *CSS McRae.* Sent to *CSS Saint Philip* hospital ship from 16
> November 1861 to 20 December 1861 for fever.

Roberts, William
>   Seaman. Gunners Mate
>   *CSS McRae. CSS Arctic,* 1862-1864.

Roche, William A.
>   Ordinary Seaman. Landsman.
>   *CSS McRae. CSS Selma,* 1862.

Rogan, John
>   Landsman.
>   *CSS McRae. CSS Pontchartrain,* 1862-1863.

Ryan, John
>   Seaman.
>   *CSS McRae.* Battle of Forts Jackson and Saint Philip (wounded in arm), 24 April 1862.

Ryan, William
>   Seaman.
>   *CSS McRae.* Battle of Forts Jackson and Saint Philip (wounded), 24 April 1862. *CSS Savannah,* 1862-1863.

Sampson, John
>   Landsman.
>   *CSS McRae.*

Sedamsky, Robert
>   Ordinary Seaman.
>   *CSS McRae.*

Seymour, Henry
>   Seaman.
>   *CSS McRae.* Battle of Forts Jackson and Saint Philip (killed), 24 April 1862.

Shaw, Alexander
>   Seaman.
>   *CSS McRae.* Sent to *CSS Saint Philip* hospital ship on 30 October 1861 for fever.

Sidney, John E.
>   Born in Louisiana
>   Second Class Boy.
>   *CSS McRae.* Sent to *CSS Saint Philip* hospital ship from 20 November 1861 to 3 January 1862 for fever. Admitted to *CSS Saint Philip* hospital ship on 6 January 1862 for fever. Discharged from navy on 8 February 1862 for fever.

Silough, Alvaro
>   Seaman.
>   *CSS McRae.*

Silvey, James
>   Seaman.
>   *CSS McRae.*

Simpson, Charles
>   Ordinary Seaman.
>   *CSS McRae.*

Smith, Edwin
>   Landsman. Seaman.
>   *CSS McRae.* CSS North Carolina, 1864.

Smith, George G.
>   Landsman.
>   *CSS McRae.* Deserted February 1862. Returned to *CSS McRae*, 13 February 1862.

Smith, James F.
>   Landsman.
>   *CSS McRae.*

Stanford, George
>   Second Class Fireman
>   *CSS McRae.* Mobile Station, 1862.

Steward, Alexander
>   Landsman.
>   *CSS McRae. CSS Florida*, 1862. *CSS Clarence, CSS Tacony, CSS Archer* Expedition, 1863 (captured 27 June 1863). Released 25 January 1865.

Tart, Thomas
>   Landsman.
>   *CSS McRae.*

Taylor, Charles
>   Seaman. Second Class Fireman.
>   *CSS McRae. CSS Rappahannock*, 1864. *CSS Tuscaloosa.*

Thomas, Frederick
>   Seaman.
>   *CSS McRae.*

Tolly, James
> Seaman.
> *CSS McRae.*

Troy, Richard
> Seaman.
> *CSS McRae.*

Tugenson, Martin
> Ordinary Seaman
> *CSS McRae.*

Usher, James W.
> Seaman
> *CSS McRae.*

Verner, Wilders
> First Class Boy.
> *CSS McRae.*

Volger, John
> Landsman.
> *CSS McRae.*

Walter, Thomas
> Coal Heaver.
> *CSS McRae.* Sent to *CSS Saint Philip* hospital ship from 24 November 1861 to 28 November 1861 for fever.

Webster, William
> Landsman.
> *CSS McRae.*

Welch, James
> Ordinary Seaman.
> *CSS McRae.* Apprehended by New Orleans Police, 30 January 1862. Returned to *CSS McRae.* Battle of Forts Jackson and Saint Philip (wounded in side), 24 April 1862.

Welsh, John
> Landsman.
> *CSS McRae. CSS General Bragg,* 1862. Attack on *USS Cincinatti* (mortally wounded), 10 May 1862. Died 13 May 1862.

White, John
> Seaman.
> *CSS McRae.* Sent to *CSS Saint Philip* hospital ship on 20 December 1861 for fever. *CSS Arctic,* 1862-1864.

Wilson, William E.
>Seaman. Ship's Steward, 9 November 1861. Disrated,
>1 April 1862.
>*CSS McRae. CSS Arctic*, 1862-1864.

Wynkoop, Abner
>Landsman.
>*CSS McRae.*

Young, Thomas
>Ordinary Seaman. Seaman.
>*CSS McRae.* Sent to Marine Hospital, New Orleans, on
>25 April 1862 for contusion.

Enlisted Marines

Aherns, Lewis C.
>Born in Virginia
>Private, 3 May 1861. Corporal, 3 August 1861.
>New Orleans Station, 1861. *CSS McRae.* Battle of Forts Jackson
>and Saint Philip, 24 April 1862. Transferred to *CSS Louisiana*,
>25 April 1862.

Bow, Michael
>Born in Ireland
>Private, 3 May 1861. Master at Arms. Private.
>*CSS McRae.* Battle of Forts Jackson and Saint Philip,
>24 April 1862. Transferred
>to CSS Louisiana, 25 April 1862. Captured and paroled. *CSS
>Richmond*, 1862. Drewery's Bluff, 1862-1864. *CSS Tallahassee*,
>1864. Fort Fisher, North Carolina, 1864-1865. First Battle
>of Fort Fisher, 23-27 December 1864. Second Battle of Fort
>Fisher (mortally wounded and captured), 15 January 1865. Died
>17 January 1865.

Bracklen, John
>Born in Ireland
>Private, 4 May 1861. Corporal.
>On roll as John Bracklin as private at New Orleans Station, 1861.
>*CSS McRae.* Battle of Forts Jackson and Saint Philip, 24 April
>1862. Transferred to *CSS Louisiana*, 25 April 1862. Jackson
>Station, 1862. *CSS Richmond*, 1863-1864. Drewery's Bluff, 1864.

Burnham, John
>   Private, 4 May 1861.
>   *CSS McRae.*

Burns, James
>   Born in England
>   Private, 4 May 1861. Corporal.
>   New Orleans Station, 1861. *CSS McRae.* Battle of Forts Jackson
>   and Saint Philip, 24 April 1862. Transferred to *CSS Louisiana*,
>   25 April 1862. *CSS Drewery*, 1863. Drewery's Bluff, 1863.

Canovan, Timothy
>   Born in Massachusetts
>   Private, 11 April 1861.
>   *CSS McRae*, 1861. Pensacola Marine Battalion, 1861. Deserted
>   to Union forces in Fort Pickens, 22 December 1861. Took Oath
>   of Allegiance 26 January 1862 and released from Union control
>   to return to Massachusetts.

Carlin, William
>   Private, 3 May 1861.
>   *CSS McRae.* New Orleans Station, 1861-1862.

Cogan, John
>   Private, 23 April 1861.
>   New Orleans Station, 1861. *CSS McRae.* Battle of Forts Jackson
>   and Saint Philip, 24 April 1862. Transferred to *CSS Louisiana*,
>   25 April 1862.

Corcoran, Bartley
>   Born in Massachusetts
>   Private, 16 April 1861.
>   New Orleans Station, 1861. *CSS McRae.* Battle of Forts Jackson
>   and Saint Philip, 24 April 1862. Transferred to *CSS Louisiana*,
>   25 April 1862. Captured and paroled. *CSS Dalman*, 1862. *CSS
>   Richmond*, 1862. *CSS Gallego*, 1864. Point Lookout Command
>   Operation, 1864. On rolls with Company B as a private from
>   March 1863 to December 1864. Reported as dead on muster
>   roll for December 1864.

Corcoran, Daniel
>   Private, 22 April 1861.
>   *CSS McRae.*

Gafany, Frank
> Private, 15 April 1861.
> *CSS McRae.* Deserted and enlisted in 13ᵗʰ LA Infantry, Company C. Pardoned for desertion on 27 August 1863 by Presidential Proclamation. Drewery's Bluff, 1863-1864.

Holt, Randolph
> Drummer
> *CSS McRae,* 1862.

James, Albert W.
> Born in Virginia
> Private, 10 April 1861. Corporal, 2 August 1861.
> Orderly Sergeant.
> New Orleans Station, 1861. *CSS McRae.* Battle of Forts Jackson and Saint Philip, 24 April 1862. Transferred to *CSS Louisiana,* 25 April 1862. *CSS Dalman,* 1862. Drewery's Bluff, 1862-1864. *CSS Drewry,* 1864. *CSS Gallego,* 1864. *CSS Richmond,* 1865. Semmes' Naval Brigade, 1865. Paroled at Greensboro, North Carolina, 26 April 1865.

Martin, Patrick
> Private, 23 April 1861
> *CSS McRae,* 1861.

Morgan, John
> Private, 17 April 1861. Sergeant, 23 April 1861.
> *CSS McRae,* 1861.

Nelson, Henry (age 22 in 1861)
> Born in Sweden
> Private, 3 May 1861.
> New Orleans Station, 1861. *CSS McRae.* Battle of Forts Jackson and Saint Philip, 24 April 1862. Transferred to *CSS Louisiana,* 25 April 1862.

Norton, William
> Private, 18 April 1861.
> New Orleans Station, 1861. *CSS McRae.* Sent to *CSS Saint Philip* hospital ship from 5 December 1861 to 20 December 1861 for tonsillitis. Battle of Forts Jackson and Saint Philip, 24 April 1862. Transferred to *CSS Louisiana,* 25 April 1862.

O'Brien, Hugh
>Private.
>*CSS McRae.*

O'Meally, Martin (age 24 in 1861)
>Born in Ireland
>Private, 3 May 1861.
>New Orleans Station, 1861. *CSS McRae.* Battle of Forts Jackson and Saint Philip, 24 April 1862. Transferred to *CSS Louisiana*, 25 April 1862.

Rivas, Charles
>Private 22 April 1861.
>New Orleans Station, 1861. *CSS McRae.* Battle of Forts Jackson and Saint Philip (severely wounded), 24 April 1862.

Seymour, John W. (age 21 in 1861)
>Born in Delaware (Wilmington)
>Private, 14 April 1861. Corporal, 23 April 1861. Sergeant, 3 August 1861. Private.
>New Orleans Station, 1861. *CSS McRae.* Battle of Forts Jackson and Saint Philip, 24 April 1862. Transferred to *CSS Louisiana*, 25 April 1862. *CSS Richmond*, 1862. *CSS Charleston*, 1863-1864.

Sparrow, Thomas
>Born in England
>Private, 20 April 1861.
>New Orleans Station, 1861. *CSS McRae.* Battle of Forts Jackson and Saint Philip, 24 April 1862. Transferred to *CSS Louisiana*, 25 April 1862.

Trowbridge, Newman. (age 22 in 1861)
>Born in Louisiana
>Private, 20 April 1861.
>*CSS McRae.* Sent to *CSS Saint Philip* hospital ship on 30 October 1861 for fever. Discharged from navy on 8 February 1862 for intermittent fever.

Whelan, John
>Private, 19 April 1861.
>*CSS McRae*, 1861-1862.

Ranks of the Confederate Navy

Commissioned Officers

1. Admiral
2. Rear Admiral
3. Commodore
4. Captain
5. Commander
6. First Lieutenant
7. Lieutenant
8. Chief Engineer
9. Surgeon
10. Paymaster

Warrant Officers

1. Master
2. Second Master in the line of Promotion
3. Passed Midshipman
4. Midshipman
5. Boatswain
6. Gunner
7. Master's Mate, if warranted
8. Assistant Surgeon
9. First Assistant Engineer
10. Second Assistant Engineer
11. Third Assistant Engineer
12. Carpenter
13. Sailmaker
14. Paymaster's Clerk
15. Captain's Clerk

Petty Officers

1. Master's Mate, not warranted
2. Mater-at-arms
3. Yeoman
4. Schoolmaster
5. Surgeon's Steward
6. Ship's Steward
7. Ship's Corporal
8. Armorer
9. Cooper
10. Ship's Cook
11. Boatswain's Mate
12. Gunner's Mate
13. Carpenter's Mate
14. Sailmaker's Mate
15. Coxswain to the squadron commander
16. Quartermaster
17. Quarter Gunner
18. Coxswain
19. Captain of Forecastle
20. Captain of Maintop
21. Captain of Foretop
22. Captain of Afterguard
23. Captain of Hold
24. Captain of Mizzentop
25. First Class Fireman
26. Painter
27. Master of Band
28. Steward to the squadron commander
29. Armorer's Mate
30. Cabin Steward
31. Wardroom Steward
32. Cabin Cook
33. Wardroom Cook

Lower Enlisted Ranks

1. Seaman
2. Second Class Fireman
3. Ordinary Seaman
4. Coal Heaver
5. Landsman
6. Boy

Ranks of the Confederate Marine Corps
Officer Ranks

1. Colonel
2. Lieutenant Colonel
3. Major
4. Captain
5. First Lieutenant
6. Second Lieutenant

Enlisted Ranks

1. Sergeant Major
2. Quartermaster Sergeant
3. Sergeant
4. Corporal
5. Private
6. Drummer
7. Fifer
8. Principal Musician
9. Musician

BIBLIOGRAPHY

Newspapers

Belmont Chronicle.
Burlington Free Press.
Charleston Mercury.
Clarksville Chronicle.
Daily Richmond Examiner.
Gallipolis Journal.
Galveston Tri-Weekly News.
Harper's Weekly.
Hartford Daily Courant.
Keowee Courior.
Memphis Daily Appeal.
Nashville Union and American.
New Orleans Bulletin.
New Orleans Daily Crescent.
New Orleans Daily Picayune.
New York Daily Tribune.
New York Herald.
New York Times.
Philadelphia Inquirer.
Richmond Daily Dispatch.
Shreveport Daily News.
The Athens Post.
The Daily True Delta.
The Shreveport Weekly News.
The Wisconsin Daily Patriot.
Vermont Phoenix.
Weekly Gazette and Comet.

Memoirs and Letters

Bacon, Edward Woolsey Papers, 1861-1865. Manuscript Collections, American Antiquarian Society.

Barlett, John Russell. "The *Brooklyn* at the Passage of the Forts". *Battles and Leaders of the Civil War Vol. 2: The Struggle Intensifies*. New York: The Century Co, 1887. 760 pp.

Blanding, Stephen F. *Recollections of a Sailor Boy: or Cruise of the Gunboat Louisiana*. Providence, RI. E.A. Johnson, 1886. 330 pp.

Davis, Jefferson. *The Rise and Fall of the Confederate Government: Volume Two*. New York: Appleton and Co., 1881. 714 pp.

Dawson, Francis W. *Reminisces of Confederate Service 1861 – 1865*. Charleston, SC: New and Courier Book Press, 1882, 212 pp.

Dawson, Sarah Morgan. *A Confederate Girl's Diary*. Boston: Riverside Press, 1913, 441 pp.

Dewey, George. *Autobiography of George Dewey: Admiral of the Navy*. New York: Charles Scribner's Sons, 1913, 337 pp.

Gift, George W., "The Story of the Arkansas," *Southern Historical Society Papers*, (Richmond, VA, 1887), Vol. 12, 116.

Gusley, Henry O. *The Southern Journey of a Civil War Marine: The Illustrated Note-Book of Henry O. Gusley*. Edited by Edward T. Cotham Jr., Austin, TX: University of Texas Press, 2006, 213 pp.

Hill, Frederic Stanhope. *Twenty Years at Sea*. Riverside Press, 1893. 273pp.

John Horry Dent, Jr., Letters, University Libraries Division of Special Collections, The University of Alabama.

Kell, John M. *Recollections of a Naval Life: Including the Cruises of the Confederate States Steamers, "Sumter" and "Alabama"*. Washington, DC: Neale Co, 1900, 307 pp.

Lee, Robert E. *The Wartime Papers of Robert E. Lee*. Boston: Little, Brown and Co, 1961, 994pp.

Mahan, Alfred T. *The Gulf and Inland Waters*. New York: Charles Scribner's Sons, 1883. 236 pp.

Morgan, James Morris. *Recollections of a Rebel Reefer*. New York: Houghton Mifflin Co, 1917. 491 pp.

Pollard, Edward A. *The Southern History of the War: Volume 1*. New York: C.B. Richardson, 1866, 657 pp.

Porter, David D. "The Opening of the Lower Mississippi". *Battles and Leaders of the Civil War Vol. 2: The Struggle Intensifies.* New York: The Century Co, 1887. 760 pp.

Read, Charles W., "Reminisces of the Confederate States Navy", *Southern Historical Society Papers*, (Richmond, VA, 1876), Vol. 1.

Robertson, William B. "The Water-Battery at Fort Jackson". *Battles and Leaders of the Civil War Vol. 2: The Struggle Intensifies.* New York: The Century Co, 1887. 760 pp.

Semmes, Raphael. *Memoirs of Service Afloat: During the War Between the States.* Baltimore, MD: Kelly Piet & Co, 1868, 833 pp.

Safford, Moses. *The Civil War Naval Diary of Moses Safford, USS Constellation.* Edited by Lawrence J. Bopp and Stephen R. Bockmiller. Charleston, SC: History Press, 2004. 379 pp.

Tenney, W.J. *The Military and Naval History of the Rebellion in the United States.* New York: Appleton and Co., 1866. 843pp.

Tomb, James H. *Engineer in Gray: Memoirs of Chief Engineer James H. Tomb.* Edited by R. Thomas Campbell. Jefferson, NC: McFarland and Co., 2005. 206 pp.

Warley, A.F. "The Ram *Manassas* at the Passage of the New Orleans Forts". *Battles and Leaders of the Civil War Vol. 2: The Struggle Intensifies.* New York: The Century Co, 1887. 760 pp.

Wilkinson, John. *The Narrative of a Blockade Runner.* New York: Sheldon & Co, 1877. 252 pp.

Government Publications

Acceptances, Applications, Appointments, Discharges, Dismissals, Oaths of Office, Resignations, Revoked Commissions. (National Archives Microfilm Publication M1991, rolls 19-20); Military Service in the Confederate Navy and Marine Corps, 1861-1865; National Archives Building, Washington, DC.

Complements, Rolls, Lists of Persons Serving in or with Vessels or Stations. (National Archives Microfilm Publication M1091, rolls 16-18); Military Service in the Confederate Navy and Marine Corps, 1861-1865; National Archives Building, Washington, DC.

Confederate States of America Navy Department. *Ordnance Instructions for the Confederate States Navy Relating to the Preparation of Vessels of War for Battle, to the Duties of Officers and Others when at*

Quarters, to the Ordnance and Ordnance Stores, and to Gunnery. 3rd ed. London: Saunders, Otley, and Company, 1864. 171 pp.

Dictionary of American Naval Fighting Ships. Navy Department, Office of the Chief of Naval Operations, Naval History Division, 1959-1981.

Journal of the Congress of the Confederate States of America, 1861-1865. Washington D.C.

Official Records of the Union and Confederate Navies in the War of the Rebellion. Washington, D.C.: Government Printing Office, 1884 – 1927

Official Records of the War of the Rebellion. Washington, D.C.: Government Printing Office, 1884 – 1927.

Regulations for the Navy of the Confederate States. 1862. Richmond, Virginia: Macfarlane and Fergusson, 1862.

Ship Register and Enrollments of New Orleans of New Orleans, Louisiana. Volume 6, 1861-1870. Baton Rouge, Louisiana: LSU Press, 1942.

United States Naval War Records Office. Register of Officers of the Confederate States Navy 1861 – 1865. Washington D.C. US Government Printing Office, 1931. 220 pp.

Illustrations (in order of appearance)

"Photo NH 48178" Photograph. From United States Naval Historical Center.

Bufford, John H. "Moon Light View of the Action off Anton Lizardo, March 6th, 1860" Lithograph. From Yale University Art Gallery: Mabel Brady Garvan Collection.

Abbot, Henry L. "Department of the Gulf. Map No. 5. Approaches to New Orleans" Map. Plate 90, Map 1. From Atlas to Accompany the Official Records of the Union and Confederate Armies. Washington, D.C.: Government Printing Office, 1895.

"Photo NH 46483" Photograph. From United States Naval Historical Center.

"Photo NH 66631" Line Engraving. From United States Naval Historical Center.

"Commander A.F. Warley" Drawing. From Battles and Leaders of the Civil War Vol. 4. New York: The Century Co, 1887. p. 641.

"Before He Swam to Liberty – Alexander and His Fellow-Captives in Fort Warren" Photograph. From The Photographic History of the Civil

War, Volume Seven: Prisons and Hospitals. New York: Review of Reviews Co., 1911, p. 139.

Popular Science Monthly. Volume Six. New York: D. Appleton and Company, 1875. p. 442.

"Photo NH 63878" Photograph. From United States Naval Historical Center.

Morgan, James Morris. *Recollections of a Rebel Reefer.* New York: Houghton Mifflin Co, 1917. p. 126.

Dudley, William. *Going South: US Naval Officer Resignations and Dismissals on the Eve of the Civil War.* Washington D.C.: Naval Historical Foundation, 1981. p. 11.

Official Records of the Union and Confederate Navies in the War of the Rebellion. Series 1, Volume 18. Washington, D.C.: Government Printing Office, 1884 – 1927. p. 345.

Official Records of the Union and Confederate Navies in the War of the Rebellion. Series 1, Volume 18. Washington, D.C.: Government Printing Office, 1884 – 1927. Front-Piece.

"Photo NH 55004-KN" Sketch. From United States Naval Historical Center.

"Photo NH 59012" Sketch. From United States Naval Historical Center.

Official Records of the Union and Confederate Navies in the War of the Rebellion. Series 1, Volume 16. Washington, D.C.: Government Printing Office, 1884 – 1927. p. 636.

"General M. Jeff Thompson" Drawing. From *Battles and Leaders of the Civil War Vol. 1.* New York: The Century Co, 1887. p. 452.

"Map Showing the System of Rebel Fortifications on the Mississippi River at Island No. 10 and New Madrid." Map. Plate 10, Map 1. From Atlas to Accompany the Official Records of the Union and Confederate Armies. Washington, D.C.: Government Printing Office, 1895.

"Docks of New Madrid, Missouri" Drawing. From *Battles and Leaders of the Civil War Vol. 1.* New York: The Century Co, 1887. p. 441.

"Photo NH 63376" Photograph. From United States Naval Historical Center.

Scharf, J. Thomas. *History of the Confederate States Navy.* New York: Rogers & Sherwood, 1887. p. 300.

Brady, Matthew. Photographer. "Admiral David G. Farragut, ca. 1860 – ca 1865" Photograph. From The National Archives Record Group 111.

Harper's Weekly, May 17, 1862.

"Portrait of Maj. Gen. Mansfield Lovell, officer of the Confederate Army" Photograph. From The Library of Congress. Call Number LC-B813- 2010 A [P&P] LOT 4213.

"Brigadier General Johnson Duncan" Drawing. From *Battles and Leaders of the Civil War Vol. 2.* New York: The Century Co, 1887. p. 35.

"Fort Jackson" Drawing. From *Battles and Leaders of the Civil War Vol. 2.* New York: The Century Co, 1887. p. 34.

"Main deck of a mortar schooner used in the bombardment of the forts Jackson and St. Philip in April, 1862" Photograph. From the United States Army Military History Institute.

"David Dixon Porter" Photograph. From *The Photographic History of the Civil War, Volume Six: The Navies.* New York: Review of Reviews Co., 1911, p. 195.

Official Records of the Union and Confederate Navies in the War of the Rebellion. Series 1, Volume 18. Washington, D.C.: Government Printing Office, 1884 – 1927. p. 287.

"Commander John K. Mitchell" Drawing. From *Battles and Leaders of the Civil War Vol. 2.* New York: The Century Co, 1887. p. 38.

Official Records of the Union and Confederate Navies in the War of the Rebellion. Series 1, Volume 18. Washington, D.C.: Government Printing Office, 1884 – 1927. p. 277.

"Porter's Mortar Schooner Firing" Drawing. From *Battles and Leaders of the Civil War Vol. 2.* New York: The Century Co, 1887. p. 32.

"Photo NH 1734" Photograph. From United States Naval Historical Center.

"Birds-Eye View of the Passage of the Forts Below New Orleans, April 24, 1862. The Second Division in Action, 4:15 A.M." Drawing. From *Battles and Leaders of the Civil War Vol. 2.* New York: The Century Co, 1887. p. 40.

"*U.S.S. Brooklyn*, the Old Ship" Photograph. From The Library of Congress.

"*USS Iroquois*" Photograph. From United States Naval Historical Center.

"Captain Thomas Craven." Drawing. From *Battles and Leaders of the Civil War Vol. 2.* New York: The Century Co, 1887. p. 61.

"*CSS Manassas* engages *USS Brooklyn*." Drawing. From *Battles and Leaders of the Civil War Vol. 2.* New York: The Century Co, 1887. p. 66.

"New Orleans City Hall." Drawing. From *Battles and Leaders of the Civil War Vol. 2.* New York: The Century Co, 1887. p. 94.

INDEX

K

L

M